MEASURING MANAGEMENT PERFORMANCE

A DEVELOPMENTAL APPROACH FOR TRAINERS AND CONSULTANTS

Terence Jackson

KOGAN
PAGE

NICHOLS/GP
PUBLISHING

Kogan Page, London   Nichols/GP Publishing, New York

First published in 1991

Apart from any fair dealing for the purposes of research or private study, or criticism or review, as permitted under the Copyright, Designs and Patents Act, 1988, this publication may only be reproduced, stored or transmitted, in any form or by any means, with the prior permission in writing of the publishers, or in the case of reprographic reproduction in accordance with the terms of licences issued by the Copyright Licensing Agency. Enquiries concerning reproduction outside those terms should be sent to the publishers at the undermentioned address:

Kogan Page Limited
120 Pentonville Road
London N1 9JN

© Terence Jackson, 1991

British Library Cataloguing in Publication Data
A CIP record for this book is available from the British Library.
ISBN 0 74940 248 2

First published in the USA in 1991 by
Nichols/GP Publishing
11 Harts Lane, East Brunswick
NJ 08816 USA

Library of Congress Cataloging-in-Publication Data
Jackson, Terence, 1952–
    Measuring management performance: a developmental approach
for trainers and consultants / Terence Jackson.
        p.   cm.
    ISBN 0-89397-411-0 : $42.95
    1. Executives—Rating of. 2. Executives—Training of. I. Title.
HD38.2.J32   1991
658.4′07125—dc20   90-26982
                                                           CIP

Typeset by BookEns Limited, Baldock, Herts
Printed and bound in Great Britain by Biddles Ltd, Guildford

MEASURING
MANAGEMENT
PERFORMANCE

*To Sheelagh,
Richard and Sarah*

Contents

Preface

This is a book for training and development professionals who want to look more closely at the measurement of management performance. It is also a book that presents a specific framework for thinking about management performance.

Measurement is an important tool for understanding what managers do, how job performance varies from manager to manager, and how it changes over time. It is also a tool which aids understanding of management strengths and weaknesses, and of areas which need development. Those professionals – trainers, developers and consultants – who help managers develop and manage better, require an understanding of how to measure management performance. This book provides that understanding by carefully blending theory which pertains to management and management practice. Unfortunately there are no easy answers and no easy solutions to the problem of performance measurement. The importance of considering some of the theoretical bases of measurement and those things we are attempting to measure, namely management performance, cannot be stressed enough.

Organizations depend on the performance of their managers to ensure productivity and profitability. The way managers perform their jobs affects operational results, and in turn affects the achievement of corporate objectives. The way managers undertake their jobs and what they do to achieve results are key issues in organizations and in management theory. To understand these matters some understanding is required of the factors which lead to successful results – the process of management, and what it means to be a successful manager.

To develop managers' performance requires some understanding of how we know when managers are performing better than they did prior to the development programme!

But this text goes further than this and looks at measurement as a development tool in its own right. This is because the view expressed here is that scientific methods should be used to clarify a situation by starting from common sense and progressing to a deeper and fuller understanding of the way people perform. Rather than abstracting or theorizing to a point where the theory bears no relation to the practical world, social and behavioural science should exist to help people learn about themselves.

Psychology and social science in general is often accused of stating the obvious by using jargon and mystification. There may be a case for the physical sciences (which the social sciences often try to unsuccessfully emulate) to generate a special terminology where scientists largely communicate with only one another. In the social sciences there is an implied relationship between the scientist and his or her 'subjects' – people. Subjects are not the inanimate objects dealt with in the physical sciences. There is a need to build on people's (the subjects') understanding, rather than abstract from it.

However, there *is* a need to explain things that are not accurately reflected by common sense alone. This requires methodologies to transcend the obvious, to dig and unearth the 'deep structure' of human action. It is the job of trainers, developers and consultants to grasp these methodologies and to facilitate the process of management learning.

This text is therefore a practical approach to the application of the science of human performance to management practice, taking up the following issues which are of central importance to management developers.

Section One of the text looks at the relationship between the theory of measurement and management practice, and why managers (and for that matter management developers) should concern themselves with theory when they have a practical day-to-day job to do. It puts the measurement of performance into context by looking at a practical scientific approach to measurement. Although this subject may look a bit intimidating at first, it takes a 'user friendly' view of the relationship between theory and management practice. The underlying assumption is that measurement exists to clarify and help managers to manage.

Within this section, Chapter 1 looks at the various criteria for a science of measurement which is both grounded in the appropriate theory and can be operationalized and used in practice.

Chapter 2 looks at an analytical structure in which to fit measurement, concentrating on those things which can be measured and the underlying theory behind them.

Chapter 3 gets down to some of the detail of measurement, starting from measurement strategy and looking at practical approaches to making measurement effective, and actually developing a measurement instrument.

Section Two then looks at how management performance is currently measured and what aspects of management performance should be taken into account. It focuses on existing practice, looking at various aspects and areas in which managers perform.

Within this section, Chapter 4 looks at the nature of management and Chapter 5 looks at management competencies and the current debate in this area, focusing on leadership as a management competency. Both chapters finish by looking at methods which the reader can use to determine what a manager does in the organization, and how competencies can be measured.

Chapter 6 then goes on to look at the roles of culture and style in management performance, focusing on the 'rules' of management and giving practical methods for measuring organizational culture and management styles (a subject which is returned to in Chapter 8).

Chapter 7 discusses the significant impact of motivation on management performance. This chapter provides useful practical advice on measuring motivation.

Section Three examines an approach to measurement – still in its early stages – which focuses on communication within an organization as a major factor in both management performance and in successful measurement. Some of the problems of trying to measure particular styles of management are looked at, within particular organizational climates where there is generally poor communication. The approach is offered not as an ultimate solution, but as a way of looking at measurement within an organization and as a way of viewing management: what is referred to continually in the text as an 'analogy'. If an analogy or 'representation' of reality can be constructed which is acceptable within an organization, and which facilitates agreement and a sharing of information, then measurement can be successful and communication – the key management performance factor – can be improved.

With these aims, Chapter 8 concentrates on the fundamental cultural and stylistic dimension of management performance.

Chapter 9 then develops this by looking at the way communication fits into the model, providing a process or developmental dimension. Methods are discussed for measuring management along these two dimensions, and the management analysis questionnaire (MAQ) is presented as an example of a measurement instrument which seeks to measure management along the two dimensions discussed.

This book is a careful mixture of theory and practice: both open-ended questions about measurement and management performance are asked, as well as practical methods for measuring performance. As such, it is an ideal 'fundamental' text for considering basic theory, it facilitates a starting point for a more advanced study of this important theory, and, as an 'operational' work, it provides a resource with which trainers and consultants can start to successfully get the measure of management performance.

SECTION ONE

THEORY INTO PRACTICE

There is nothing so practical as good theory. (Kurt Lewin)

INTRODUCTION

Measurement is not an end in itself. It is a way of representing certain aspects of human action in a very abstract and codified way. It is based on particular theories about the way people should act, and about how actions can be studied scientifically. For practical managers it is a way of looking at performance to clarify problems and to help them manage more effectively.

We start by looking at the role of theory and the way that a scientific approach may be put to practical use.

What good is theory to management practice? How can theories benefit managers who have to work at a practical level to solve day-to-day problems? This Section seeks to answer these questions by looking at some very fundamental issues of what 'theory' is, how it relates to the world of the manager and how the two may be connected to enable the trainer or consultant to help the manager manage better.

1 The Importance of Theory to Management Practice

Measurement is a 'scientific' idea. It conjures up ideas of precision. Can we apply the ideas of measurement to human performance and can we talk about a 'science' of management performance? These questions may seem far removed from the day-to-day work of the manager, but understanding the importance of theory to management practice is a key element within this text. The aim of this first chapter is to try to answer the questions: what is a science of human performance, and how does this relate to the practice of management?

SCIENCE AND COMMON SENSE

Let us start at the beginning with an idea of what we are talking about: a definition of terms. A *theory* is ' a system of rules, procedures and assumptions used to produce a result' (*Collins Dictionary Of The English Language*).

But how does this differ from common sense? It only does this when the theory is placed within a systematic body of knowledge and methodology for generating and validating this knowledge – namely as a 'science'. It is science which tells us something which common sense does not, which enables us to produce results (as the definition above suggests) which we would not otherwise produce.

What does common sense not tell us? What are we missing by relying on common sense alone? Harré, Clarke and De Carlo (1985) point out that certain processes are 'hidden' from our immediate experience, usually by virtue of their magnitude (too small or too large) or their pace (too quick or too slow), at least in the physical and natural sciences. It is the job of science to 'discover' what is hidden, to draw it into the realms of our understanding, to gain advantage from this knowledge.

Unfortunately, the science of human action still operates at a fairly basic level, often not helping our understanding, as the following will illustrate.

Day follows night. Wherever there is day, so there is night. There is a strong correlation between the two. In the social sciences, researchers look for a strong correlation between two or more events, to indicate a possible causal relationship. For example, where a certain training programme is introduced into an organization, there is a corresponding increase in performance of staff: there is a strong correlation between the two. There is therefore a good chance that the training programme 'causes' the increase in performance.

This may be looking at things a bit simplistically, since where possible the researcher will look for other factors which might also have an impact on the performance of staff in this instance. The principle is the same, however. If B follows A consistently, a good assumption can be made that A probably causes B.

Let us go back to the example of day and night. If we apply the same criterion to day following night, there is a good chance that night *causes* day (or day causes night)! Of course it does not, but why not?

The classical and medieval scholars, from Ptolemy to Copernicus, thought that there was more to the passage of day and night and that of the seasons than met the eye. A hypothesis (a theory) was developed of the structural and 'processional' nature of the universe. A conceptual leap in the dark was taken. The task was then to demonstrate that this theory was correct. By careful and detailed observation over an extended period of time, the theory held true as an explanation for the position and motion of our planet (Hurd and Kipling, 1964, is a useful source for further elaboration on these theories).

This brief diversion into astronomy does illustrate some important points. Firstly, common sense is often sound but may miss a lot of what constitutes the reality of a situation. Thus, it may have been common sense to regard the world as flat, but was this the reality of the situation?

Secondly, and returning to social and behaviour science, these disciplines do not necessarily take on board common-sense views, and may try to offer explanations which at best do not offer any additional explanation of events or things, and at worst may confuse the issue.

This is not to tar all social science with the same brush, but to merely point out that if we were to apply certain methods of the social sciences to an explanation of day followed by night we may well come up with the answer that night causes day. This is a plausible explanation in the 'positivist' approaches which predominate in the social and behavioural sciences; see, for example, the critique in Harré (1981).

Thirdly, there may be some hidden 'deep structure' which remains to be discovered by scientific methods, and which comprises a set of 'rules' (such as the way the planets revolve around the sun) which may enable us to gain some control over the processes involved. This may be by prediction of, intervention in, or manipulation of, events (although intervention and manipulation are difficult if not impossible in the case of astronomy, and manipulation may raise moral questions in social science).

In other words, a science is not very helpful to practising managers unless it tells them something they do not already know, and unless that new information can be used in a practical way to produce results.

In the field of psychology, with which this present work is principally concerned, various attempts have been made to dig deeper, to transcend the obvious, to provide a psychological explanation of behaviour. Of note is the psycho-analytical approach of Freud which, despite continuing controversy, has had a profound influence on psychological thinking. Certain off-shoots of this thinking, for example transactional analysis (see Berne, 1964, and Harris, 1967), have contributed to the repertoire of management training programmes. Berne (1964), for example, tries to provide an understanding of the hidden rules according to which people interact, by giving an account of interpersonal relations using the analogy of playing games.

A psychology which is helpful to the practising manager must start from the basis of common sense, least of all because it will be judged initially by the manager from the standpoint of common sense – what researchers call 'face validity': see, for example, Kline (1986) and the discussion in Chapter 3. Common sense is a cognitive framework within which we view our world and the basis upon which we act. The label 'common' suggests that we might hold this framework *in* common with other people who share similar types of experiences to ourselves. However, as Reason and Rowan (1981:xii) point out, this 'naive inquiry' or day-to-day thinking is prone to error owing to our bias, prejudice and anxiety, and to pressures for group conformity. Common-sense is also largely 'uncodified' and therefore difficult to quantify; as is explained in Chapter 9).

To be at all useful to us a psychology (or any other science) must change the basis upon which we act, and demonstrate that it produces the results we require in a more effective way than simply relying on our common-sense view. To do this it must modify our cognitive framework: the way we think of and see the world. In some ways this may be seen as a radical view of science!

PSYCHOLOGY AS A CHANGE AGENT

One of the things that most sciences have been very successful in doing is generating their own jargon, and therefore creating a mystique around them to keep out the uninitiated. However, a psychology which is useful to the practising manager must *facilitate* a change in the way that person thinks of, perceives, and acts towards, the environment, to enable the achievement of results.

It must be a *change agent*, building on common sense, clarifying our understanding, facilitating our actions, and validating that experience by the achievement of the objectives of our actions.

By using the word 'facilitate' we (the budding scientists) are suggesting that in some way the subjects (ie people) of our research are involved actively. For example, if we are looking at ways in which management performance can be improved, and are building on the common-sense views of those managers by clarifying their understanding and facilitating their action, we are implying that the managers are actually making a contribution.

The fact of the matter is that whether we like it or not, when trying to study human action we are involved with the subject of our enquiry by virtue of the fact that we are human beings as well. For many years social and behavioural scientists have been trying to negate or even ignore this hurdle to 'objectivity', despite evidence from the classic Hawthorne Studies which show that by studying what human beings do, the study itself will influence the way they behave and therefore influence the results. A summary of this work can be found in Brown (1954).

If we, as human beings, conduct our scientific studies of other human beings by reference to our own common-sense views – inevitably our own value systems, bias and prejudice colour our thinking – why not also start with the common-sense views of the people whose actions we are studying?

There are obvious pitfalls to this, the expression of which can, and are, aired by common-sense views. The following will illustrate.

Suppose we are looking at the performance of managers in a particular company. Starting with the managers' own common-sense or day-to-day thinking, we might first ask them to assess their own performance. Immediately the problems of doing this spring to mind. We can list them:

- They will rate themselves more leniently than might their supervisors.

- They may rate themselves differently according to the circumstances; for example, more leniently if the assessment is related to pay than they would if related to training needs.
- They may have different views on the criteria of their performance: how it is judged.
- Different information may be available to each manager owing to variations in their supervisors' feedback, or level of seniority of the manager within the organization.
- Managers may differ in terms of different self-esteem, 'personality', regard for the company, which may colour their views and this may change according to their 'moods'.
- It may be difficult to compare the performance of one manager with another based on self-ratings: one may be more lenient than the other; they may have different perceptions of how performance is judged.

These are some of the problems. What of the reasons for including self-assessment in this exercise, and how can we improve on the common-sense views that the managers assessing themselves might have?

Firstly, we may want the exercise to facilitate change, by subsequently introducing a training programme which may increase performance. To do this, we must gain a commitment from the managers to improve their skills and apply them to increase their work performance. By involving them at an early stage in assessing their strengths and weaknesses, we are half-way to gaining a commitment if they recognize certain skills deficiencies which may be overcome by training (see, for example, McEnery and McEnery, 1987, for a discussion of self-assessment of training needs and the concurrence and commitment of self-raters).

Secondly, we may wish to discover how they are currently judging their own performance so that common agreement may be reached. If managers are pulling in different directions, this may in itself hamper performance. Tsui and Ohlott (1988) for example, identify poor inter-rater agreement as a problem. Of course it may be so within the positivist view of science discussed above, but not necessarily in the view which we are currently expounding.

Thirdly, we may wish to lay bare some of the other underlying influences on our self-raters in order to clarify the implicit rules and processes involved. We can then explore with the managers how this information may be used to improve performance.

Ways in which we may improve on common-sense thinking might

be to develop instruments (such as questionnaires) which make uniform the criteria of performance, develop understanding of the managers, and clarify what is needed to develop performance. Part of this process may indeed be to gain agreement between self-raters, and between other people rating them, for example their supervisors or their peers.

By this stage we should be able to begin to build up a picture based on a collective common sense. We should begin to get an idea of the managers' performance outside the immediate self-interest of the individual self-raters. However, up to this point have we used anything we can call a scientific method? Have we generated what might be called scientific knowledge?

Let us first discuss what is not necessarily scientific knowledge, and again take a common-sense approach to this.

We have obtained managers' self-rating, their supervisors' ratings and peer ratings of these managers' performance. We have got agreement on how to judge performance and how well managers are performing against this bench-mark. The common-sense thing to do next would be to try to find out how valid these agreed performance ratings are, and how valid the bench-mark is.

For example, let us say that we found (as indeed McEnery and McEnery, 1987, did) that the following job dimensions were important to managers, and that they were assessed on each dimension by both supervisor and by self-awarding a score:

- prioritizing;
- scheduling;
- following up;
- recognizing problems;
- gathering information;
- analysing problems;
- making decisions;
- adopting new approaches;
- co-ordinating;
- keeping up-to-date;
- achieving results;
- enforcing rules;
- writing;
- presenting verbally;
- being aware of structure;
- selecting employees;
- conducting performance reviews;

- developing subordinates;
- instructing employees;
- assigning work;
- delegating tasks;
- involving subordinates;
- handling grievances;
- maintaining good atmosphere;
- maintaining job knowledge;
- handling problem subordinates;
- providing feedback to subordinates;
- making non-discriminatory decisions;
- providing safe environment.

We can perhaps validate these criteria, and ratings given for them, by reference to the actual results of the managers. In a production environment this may be the rate and quality of production of the manager's section; in a sales department it may be the value of sales (see also Chapter 5). This should hopefully show that where managers have high ratings on the above dimensions, so they have obtained good operational results.

But again the question can be asked, is there anything scientific about this?

Firstly, a number of job dimensions (or skills elements of the job which managers have felt important) have been made explicit. This is useful, and has extended the common-sense knowledge of the managers concerned.

Secondly, scores have been given to each dimension: 1 = unsatisfactory, 2 = minimum, 3 = satisfactory, 4 = more than satisfactory, 5 = outstanding (McEnery and McEnery, 1987). Again this may be useful and draws on common-sense concepts of the raters.

Thirdly, ratings on these dimensions have been compared with operational performance (although not in McEnery and McEnery's, 1987, study quoted above). But is this not a course which enlightened commonsense would take anyway?

No, this is not science! For example, where is the theory of human action which underpins this type of analysis? (Certainly McEnery and McEnery, 1987, do not make this apparent.) This certainly does not meet our criteria of science which we can now summarize.

CRITERIA FOR A SCIENTIFIC STUDY OF MANAGEMENT PERFORMANCE

A science of management performance must:

- discover what would otherwise be hidden;
- start from common sense, be free from jargon, and be capable of practical application in an understandable way;
- be capable of changing the cognitive framework within which managers view the world and on which basis they act;
- enable managers to gain control over the processes identified – by prediction, intervention or other action – and thus enable them to produce results they would not otherwise have produced;
- take account of pressures of group conformity, prejudice, bias, cultural differences and other influences;
- be able to prove the knowledge it generates, in order to make it valid.

These would appear to be quite stringent criteria. They are certainly an extension to the positivist approach to science. They ensure that theory relates to practice, and therefore management results. In so doing, the results will verify the theory, and so science will progress in the field of human performance.

However, we are not throwing away positivist science. Let us look at this in a bit more detail since it is important.

In the example discussed above, where ratings were given for a number of managerial job dimensions, we suggested that this might be validated by reference to the actual results achieved by the manager who was rated (see also Chapter 5). By doing this we are trying to establish a relationship between high ratings on the job dimensions and good operational results.

If we found that such a correlation exists, could we assume that if a training programme were introduced to improve the skills needed to perform those particular job dimensions (prioritizing, scheduling, following up, recognizing problems, etc), there would be a corresponding improvement in operational results as ratings increased for each job dimension?

Putting this more simply, could we say there is a causal relationship between an improvement in the skills needed to do the job (cause or 'independent variable') and operational results (effect or dependent variable')?

Again this is a common-sense conclusion, but commonsense also provides a view of the pitfalls. Firstly, there may be other factors impacting on the outcome, so it is difficult to distinguish the actual 'effects' of training on operational results. Secondly, there are so many imponderables with regard to human beings, with all their quirks and foibles, that it is difficult to determine a direct link between training for skills and operational results.

We can set up a number of research designs to try to eliminate the impact of other factors on the outcome of results.

A control group research design is as follows:

'Treated' group

Test 1 ——————————— Treatment ——————————— Test 2
                      (eg training
                      programme)

'Untreated' group

Test 1 ——————————————————————————————— Test 2

A control group design will look at the performance of an 'untreated' group to see if performance has remained unaffected where the 'experimental' group has improved in performance. A time series design will introduce the training intervention between two of a whole series of performance tests to see if performance has improved between these two tests and remains the same between tests where a training intervention was not inserted (Spencer, 1986, provides a useful and straightforward account of a number of the designs).

A time series research design is as follows:

Test 1 _____ Test 2 _____ Treatment _____ Test 3 _____ Test 4

However, given the use of such designs, would we not simply be confirming what managers might already suspect – relying on their knowledge of the operational situation and their staff – that either training their staff has had an effect or it has not? Would it not be simpler to ask the managers concerned? But would they not feel 'cheated' that they have not received the 'scientific treatment' and that we (the researchers) have not done something a bit more 'objective'?

What is being suggested here is that 'positivism', or the cause-effect model, is simply a second stage after commonsense in a hierarchy that looks something like that below.

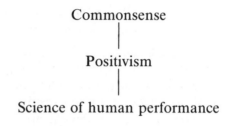

Commonsense

Positivism

Science of human performance

It is no accident that common sense has been placed at the top of the hierarchy because this is what controls the use of the other two in an organization, with science of human performance at the bottom of the hierarchy since positivism is more likely to be employed in an organization. Positivism is easier to sell in some ways since it appears closer to common sense: but it may simply give an illusion of science! We have so far laid down certain criteria for the science of human performance. What should this science look like and why is it important to management practice? We can comment on this with reference to each criterion we specified above.

Criterion 1: To be useful a science must discover what would otherwise be hidden. Harré, Clarke and De Carlo (1985) suggest a hierarchical structure of control of human actions, laid out below.

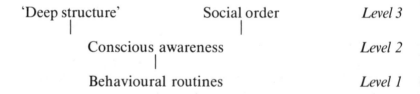

Much work in psychology has been undertaken at levels 1 and 2, but very little at level 3 which is largely hidden from consciousness. Harré, Clarke and De Carlo (1985) suggest that structure of mind and the social order have developed hand in hand, mostly through the facility of language, and that the implied rules by which level 3 controls the two lower levels are discoverable.

There is nothing mystical in this. It largely grows out of a sociological approach which is rooted in the work of Durkheim (1915). Durkheim studies the totemism of Aboriginal tribes of Australia and Indian tribes of North America (perhaps the latter provides the popular image of Red Indians dancing round a totem pole). The members of each clan (a subdivision of a tribe) was found to worship a particular animal (eg crow) which was also the name of the clan.

Durkheim maintained that the origins of the religious beliefs by which their lives were governed, were derived from the identification with the society (clan) in which they lived. This was seen to be greater and more powerful than the individual clansman. The rituals (associated with dancing round the totem pole) reinforced and drove these beliefs home. Thus the deep-seated beliefs which were acted upon unconsciously were no more than a set of implicit rules derived from the society in which the individuals lived.

Do we not act, for the most part unconsciously, upon a set of rules which are derived from our own experiences within society, which we adopt and through which we view our world? And would not our actions, and performance in an organizational setting, be easier to understand if we could discover this 'deep structure'? But how do we go about this?

Harré, Clarke and De Carlo (1985) suggest the construction of a theory (or model) which can be used as the basis for analysis and tested in practice. They suggest the use of an analogy, a representation of reality. Goffman (1959), for example, uses the analogy of a dramatical enactment to describe human action which is governed by certain 'scripts'. Berne (1964) uses a games analogy whereby points or 'strokes' are scored. Homans (1958) uses an analogy based on economic exchange where individuals' self-interest is advanced in social exchanges.

Once such an analogy is constructed to represent reality, it must be tested to make sure it works in practice.

There is nothing new about the use of analogy in science. Numbers on a clock face are an analogy of time; they are simply a way of representing reality, just as any quantitative measure of reality (voltage, IQ, personality test) is.

An analogic representation of the way people perform helps us to:

- simplify reality and make it more understandable;
- dig deeper than observable behaviour to find out the rules by which people conduct their lives;
- understand the 'structural' relations between people (the way people work together, and how they relate to the organization within which they work);
- understand belief systems within an organization which affect the way people perform.

At this stage it can be suggested that a key to digging deeper, and to clarifying and understanding that which may be hidden, is the communication which takes place between individuals. It is through communication that we understand our world and we understand ourselves. Without good feedback from a supervisor (or from customers), it is difficult to gain an understanding of our own performance at work. The better the feedback, the better the understanding.

Communication also enables us to reach agreement about the meaning of performances in our working lives. Performing within a job function not only involves using a collection of behaviours or *actions*, but it also has meaning for the individual performers as an *act*. This meaning is negotiated (not freely as some social theories such as phenomenology, eg Schutz, 1972, suggest, but within certain rules and relationships of power and influence) within an organization and between individuals, their peers and their managers.

It is through communication that we 'internalize' our social experiences, providing a reservoir of meanings about the social world and our position within that world. For many theorists (including Mead, 1934, and Goffman, 1959) this idea is encompassed within the notion of 'self', or 'self-concept' (see, for example, Burns, 1979). This is slightly different from the idea of 'personality', and we will be examining how an understanding of self-concept (and its generation through communication) is important to performance measurement. By looking at self-concept, we can dig deeper and reveal that which may be hidden from a common-sense conception of human action.

Criterion 2: To be acceptable a science must start from common sense, be free from jargon, and be capable of practical application in an understandable way. Science, as a body of information and knowledge, should be communicable. Often, communication is between scientists who share the same jargon. This is not to decry the use of specialists' terminology within subject specialisms, since a new concept may require a new body of terms. It is simply to point to a misunderstanding of the way knowledge (any knowledge, not just scientific knowledge) is communicated in society.

In communication theory (see, for example, Cherry, 1957) there is a concept of 'entropy' and 'redundancy' in the language we use. There is a lot of repetition and superfluity (redundancy) in language which makes it understandable despite the presence of 'noise' or interruption to the message, mishearing and breaking of grammatical rules to name some examples. There is very little in communication which is actually new (entropy). Anything which is new has to build on the old or redundant information.

So it is with scientific information. It has to build on what we already know. It has to introduce us to new information and concepts by carefully referring back to the known. Accepting new information is a high risk business! It has to relate to what is already acceptable. It has to be tested in practice and thus be referred back to what we have already; but must be an improvement on what we already know, to be accepted as new knowledge and not as 'hype'.

Again the use of an analogy related to common-sense knowledge is helpful here to join the old with the new. A very impressive analogy of this type is Coonradt's (1984) *The Game of Work*, where work is related to a football game with score-keeping and out of bounds rules, and which while not claiming scientific status, does provide some useful insights.

Criterion 3: A science must be capable of changing the cognitive framework within which we view the world, and on which basis we act. Scientific discoveries change our perception of the world. Copernicus, Newton, Einstein, Dalton and Rutherford, to name but a few, have changed the way we look at the world. They did this by some sort of reaction to the existing knowledge of the time: building on this knowledge but ultimately contradicting it. By a 'dialectic' process of thesis, antithesis and synthesis) current thinking is brought into question but not disposed of. Rather the new thinking is synthesized with the old. This is in line with the discussion above on redundancy and entropy and reflects similar concepts.

A science of human behaviour must not just develop out of positivism and other ideas of science in a dialectic way, but must build on common sense, often contradicting it, but synthesizing the new with the old, the every-day beliefs with the revelations of those aspects which are hidden, as below.

Science of
human performance

Positivism   Common sense

Figure 1.1 *Science and common sense*
(Compare with Reason and Rowan, 1981:xiii.)

However, a change in an aspect of our cognitive framework is not necessarily a prelude to action and results (see Criterion 4 below).

Actions may come first as part of a learning process which then provides a new way of looking at events and processes, which in turn leads on to further action and further change in perception. The stages of the following example will help to clarify this:

1. A classroom exercise is conducted in a management skills course to demonstrate the effects of lack of eye contact during a social encounter, without this objective being made explicit beforehand (action).
2. As a result of the exercise the participants realize the effects of eye contact in social encounters (change in cognitive framework).
3. The exercise is again repeated, and participants should now have better control of the encounter (action).
4. Discussion is developed to encourage participants to think about how this may be useful in work situations (change in cognitive framework).
5. When back at work participants then put this new knowledge to use in gaining control of social encounters (action).

Of course the starting point may well precede an action stage, but how much more complete a change in cognitive framework is enabled if participants can realize a new perspective through their own (directed) activities (Rogers, 1951:389, is a good start to exploring the idea of experiential learning, 'we cannot teach another person directly; we can only facilitate his learning', with Holt, 1976:7, developing the point that education is 'something a person gets for himself, not that which someone else gives or does to him').

The next criterion builds on this.

Criterion 4: When applied to human action, a science should enable us to gain control over the processes identified, by prediction, intervention or manipulation, and thus enable us to produce results we would not otherwise have produced. It may not be possible to have a 'pure' social science, but only applied social sciences! But we cannot proceed on this point without considering the preceding three criteria, and the following criteria, 5 and 6.

Criterion 5: When applied to human action by human beings (scientists), a science must take account of pressures of group conformity, prejudice, bias, cultural differences and other influences.

Criterion 6: The knowledge that a science generates must be proveable to make it valid. The approach which has come to be known as 'action research' (see, for example, Sanford, 1981, for an overview, and

Rowbottom, 1977, for an example of organizational action research) addresses some of the practical problems of validation. It was conceived by Lewin (1947) as a way of studying social actions by intervening in events and studying the effects. He drew up the following model to illustrate this process.

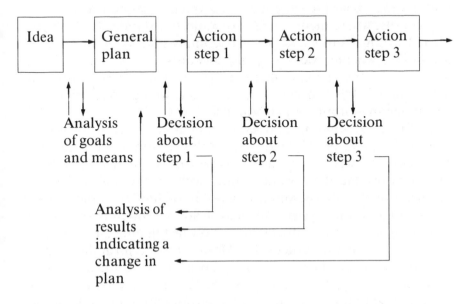

Figure 1.2 *Action research* (Adapted from Lewin, 1947)

Starting with a general idea about reaching a desired goal, the first step is to examine this idea in the context of the means available to reach the goal. Fact-finding about the situation might be needed before a plan can be developed. From a plan of how to reach the objective, a decision about the first action step emerges.

This first step must then be executed, followed by further fact-finding directed at evaluating the action to show if achievement is below or above expectation, formulating the next step, and modifying the overall plan if necessary. It also gives the planner a chance to learn and gain additional insight into strengths and weaknesses of techniques, methods and means used.

The following action steps also comprise this spiral of planning, executing and fact-finding until the objective is reached. Action research ensures the connection between theory and practice by demonstrating the practical consequences of theories which have been developed 'in the field'. It is worth staying with Lewin (1947) for a while, while turning to problems which action research methods seek to overcome.

Firstly, Lewin tells us, people who are involved in 'social management' are often denied the opportunity to satisfy their natural desire to fact-find. They are unable, in a systematic way, to gain valuable information about the situation from which they can learn.

Secondly, where there is a lack of 'objective standards of achievement' learning cannot take place. It is impossible to tell how well we are doing, whether we are going forwards or backwards, in the absence of 'criteria for evaluating the relation between effort and achievement'. We can easily come to the wrong conclusions and encourage inappropriate performance.

'Realistic fact-finding and evaluation is a prerequisite for any learning' (Lewin, 1947:334). If we refer this maxim to a line management situation, where a manager is necessarily embroiled in problems of processing the day's work, coping with operational and people problems as they occur, and acting as 'fire-fighter' on a moment-by-moment basis, with the pressures of deadlines looming on the very near horizon, it is very difficult to see how fact-finding and evaluation can form part of a manager's day. However, to perform the requisite activities of management *per se*, as opposed to the technical activities which are often part of a managers job, it is necessary to monitor, disseminate and make decisions based on information available (see, for example, the managerial roles outlined by Mintzberg, 1973). We will return to the nature of managers' jobs in Chapter 4.

The way that an approach to measuring management performance can help is to ensure that theory relates to practice in such a way that managers can employ the required techniques in their day-to-day activities. Trainers, developers and consultants should ensure that any science applied in the workplace should facilitate a manager's job rather than hinder it. It should also satisfy our criteria 4, 5 and 6 above by:

- helping managers control change;
- overcoming managers' bias and prejudice which may lead to a wrong decision;
- being valid.

Let us now take these principles and see how they apply to the construction of a framework for measuring management performance.

2 A Framework for Analysing Management Performance

So far we have discussed certain considerations for constructing a framework or model for analysing management performance, and, central to this, the relationship between theory and management practice. We have laid down certain, stringent criteria for such a scientific approach. We now begin to construct the framework which meets those criteria, which will enable us to analyse management performance. To fulfil the criteria we need to:

- discover what would otherwise be hidden (criterion 1);
- develop a practical approach which starts from common sense (criterion 2);
- change managers' accepted ways of viewing their situation where appropriate (criterion 3);
- help managers gain control of their situation and produce results they would not otherwise have produced (criterion 4);
- overcome prejudice and bias managers may have (criteria 5);
- demonstrate that the knowledge managers gain from this is valid (criterion 6).

These are general conditions we must satisfy that should relate to any human science. There are certain questions (which arise out of these criteria) which we must consider in relation to what we are trying to achieve by measuring management performance. These questions are as follows:

- What is the current common sense by which managers actions are guided (see criterion 1)?
- What is missing from this common-sense approach which prevents managers performing better (see criterion 1)?
- How can we expand on this common-sense (see criterion 2) in order to:
  - change managers' perceptions (see criterion 3);
  - help managers achieve better results (see criterion 4);
  - overcome influence of bias and subjectivity (see criterion 5)?
- How can we show that this approach is valid (see criterion 6)?

AN ANALYTICAL STRUCTURE

In order to address the above questions, and to try to satisfy the criteria for a scientific approach which we have outlined, the following analytical structure is proposed.

Firstly, there is a need to obtain an idea of the current common-sense ideas by which management actions are guided. There are a number of theoretical and practical steps which we can take to obtain this information. Chapters 4 and 5, for example, include a discussion of management activities and competencies which can be gleaned from both the academic and popular management press. These provide a distillation of current management thinking on management competencies, and those attributes and abilities which managers require to perform effectively. Other research-based activities can be carried out to obtain an idea of common-sense thinking. The current author, for example, has used Repertory Grid to elicit commonly held views about management performance ('skills language, see p. 94), and this method is described in Chapter 5. Such commonly held views as:

- communicating;
- leading;
- team working;
- delegating;
- perceptive;
- goal setting;

as well as 'lucky', 'hardworking' and other constructs, have emerged as being seen to be important to good management in one finance company. This information can then be used to 'ask the right questions' of managers in order to obtain more structured information on their perceptions of performance (satisfying criterion 2).

Secondly, methods and instruments can be devised to obtain managers' perceptions of their own performance and perceptions of their co-workers (including superiors, subordinates and peers). The actual methods used should be determined on the basis of the preliminary work on the common-sense framework of the managers, as their acceptability (face validity) will be dependent on this. These perceptions could include information about managers' motivations, attitudes and assumptions regarding performance. We can term this type of analysis *content* analysis, a term we will develop more fully later in this chapter and demonstrate in Chapter 7 (again this addresses criterion 2).

Thirdly, and in association with the second step above, an analysis should be carried out of the rules by which management performance is governed and regulated within the organizational context in which the managers work. In many cases these rules will not be written down and may be more implicit than explicit. Where these rules are largely hidden we may well be addressing criterion 1 as well as criterion 2. An analysis can be executed by gaining consensus on performance criteria based on what is valued by the organization. The present author uses ranking techniques (see Chapter 5) to determine the importance placed on certain criteria by managers and co-workers. In some cases this information can be verified or corroborated by observation and reference to such written evidence as annual appraisal forms. This type of investigation we can label *context* analysis, and we explore the concept of 'context' further in this chapter and in Chapter 6.

Fourthly, and as part of this comprehensive analysis, we can address the conduct of managers by focusing on the actions which contribute to their results. What are managers actually doing (and saying they do, along with their co-workers) which contributes to good performance as defined by the rules identified in point three above? We can term this *conduct* analysis and we take this up towards the end of this chapter (addressing criterion 2).

Fifthly, once this information is accummulated, we can then feed this back to managers – providing insight into how others see them and how others view management performance criteria – to check on perceptions and verify their own perceptions of self. Structured advice on how managers can use this information and how to act on it, particularly from the developmental point of view, is essential at this stage. Here we are addressing criterion 3 as we are attempting to change managers' views where appropriate. That is, where perceptions on performance in an organization are disparate and there is a need to draw co-workers together to facilitate more effective communication to enable a better sharing of information. These ideas will be explored more specifically in Chapters 8 and 9.

Lastly, we can assess if these changes in perception, brought about by the input of new information, change behaviour in a developmental way. This can only be achieved by monitoring performance over the longer term. Here we are addressing criterion 4.

As part of this process, validation measures and reliability checks should be built in, in order to address criterion 6 (validation), criterion

1 (discovering something which would otherwise be hidden: in this
case possible disparity in perceptions of management performance
and underlying rules about this performance), and criterion 5 (bias
and unreliability of raters in the process of performance evaluation).

We will address all these issues raised, as part of the analytical
structure proposed above, during the course of this text. We can summarize this structure as follows.

Step	Issue	Concept	Method	More information
1.	What is the current common sense which governs manage-ment action?	*Content* Perceptions Skills Language	Repertory Grid	Chapters 4 and 5
2.	How do managers see their own performance?	*Content* Competencies Managers' own perceptions	Content analysis	Chapter 7
3.	What are the rules by which managers' performance is governed?	*Context* Rules	Ranking techniques	Chapters 5 and 6
4.	What are managers actually doing?	*Conduct* Performance	Observation	Chapter 5
5.	Are managers' perceptions of self the same as others see them?	Feedback	Feed back information to managers	Chapters 8 and 9
6.	Is there any change in performance?	Development through feedback	Monitor performance	

Figure 2.1 *An analytical structure*

We can now look at some of the concepts we have referred to in

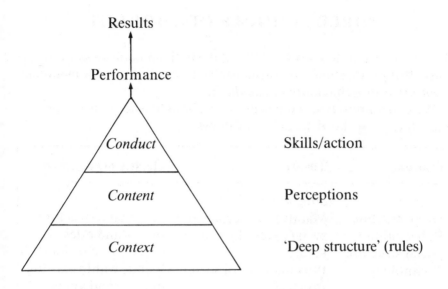

Figure 2.2 *A context–content–conduct model*

order to draw an overall picture of management performance. Schematically we can represent this as follows.

This model synthesizes three major social theories which are often seen as opposing schools of thought. The apparent antithesis between them often gets in the way of our understanding of human action when these theories are treated in a doctrinaire way. Used together they can provide a powerful conceptual model of human performance.

As in Harré, Clarke and De Carlo's (1985) hierarchical structure of control of human action (see p. 26), *context* is seen as a governing factor and a starting point for looking at performance. However, to investigate human performance it is not usually possible to start at the 'deep structure' but to start with common-sense notions at the *content* level, leading to people's perceptions of the way they act (the *conduct* level). This involves the manager's competency or wherewithall to perform. But actual performance or the doing of something according to criteria of success, is governed by the three factors of *context, content* and *conduct*. More specifically: performance is governed by the rules by which people perform, their perceptions or attitudes in terms of what is in it for them, and the skills and knowledge to actually carry out the performance.

THREE SCHOOLS OF THOUGHT

The three disparate schools of thought which an analysis of perform-ance brings together are Structuralism (*context*), Phenomenology (*content*), and Behaviourism (*conduct*).

We can summarize these schools of thought and their relation to the concepts so far discussed as follows.

Concept	Theory	Effective management
Context Deep structure Rules/culture Social structure Technology	*Structuralism* Mainly sociological and social psychological theory Pre-eminence of social structure Goals socially defined Objectives and actions are structurally driven	Understand structure Understand rules governing behaviour Operate within existing structure and know where changes are possible and desirable
Content Perceptions Motives Objectives	*Phenomenology* Mainly social philosophy and psychological theory Individuals are controllers of destiny Social meaning is negotiated	Understand others' perceptions of self and of others Understand how self and others explain events such as promotion Understand others' objectives and how these influence behaviour
Conduct Competencies Skills/behaviour	*Behaviourism* Mainly psychological Overt behaviour is primary Emphasis on skills	Understand skills required for jobs Understand the process of performance Clarify end result to which performance is addressed

Figure 2.3 *Summary of context–content–conduct theory*

We can also relate these concepts schematically to current management theory and developmental methods as follows.

Concept	Theory	Management/organizational Development
Context	*Structuralism*	Systems theory Socio-technical approaches Redesign system to improve quality of work life (QWL)
Content	*Phenomenology*	Process/action approaches Organizational development Changing culture to match individual and organizational objectives
Conduct	*Behaviourism*	Social skills training Training Other skills approaches to management development

Figure 2.4 *Context–content–conduct and development*

Let us look at the three theories of Structuralism, Phenomenology and Behaviourism, and the way in which they can be drawn together in a common methodology.

Structuralism

This term can be used very broadly to represent the various, mainly sociological and social psychological, theories which emphasize the pre-eminent influence of social structure on human actions; that human beings are not free agents but act according to the norms and rules laid down within the society and within the social organizations in which people live. Structural functionism within early British and American sociology and social anthropology (eg Parsons, 1949, and Radcliffe-Brown, 1952), and systems and open systems approaches in social psychology (eg Katz and Kahn, 1978) represent a major theme within the structuralist framework. Here, goals and the means of obtaining these goals, are socially defined by a society, or social organization, which operates 'functionally' to maintain itself and to achieve certain goals. Just like a human organism, its component parts (organs) function to maintain the whole and achieve its ends. Open systems theory recognizes the problem of regarding a social structure as a discrete entity like a human organism. A commercial organization, for example, contains many influences from the external environment through the involvement of its members in other, outside, organizations and social groups, from relations with clients, customers and suppliers.

The point of this theory is that people's objectives and actions are structurally driven, rather than structure being people driven. People's actions are defined by the roles they are given within the social structure, despite there being some room to interpret these roles by the individuals occupying them.

Structure plays an important part in management performance, and the measurement of the structural influence on performance is an issue which Likert (1967) explores, taking a systems approach which looks at the prevailing management system within an organization. The four types of management system he explores are exploitative-authoritarian, benevolent-authoritarian, consultative, and partici-pative group. By measuring organizations on a continuum across these four systems he demonstrates a connection between high performances and the participative group system.

Harré (1988) takes a different approach to understanding structural influences on performance by concentrating on the underlying structural rules by which people carry out their actions. The patterns of rules within which people perform are not necessarily obvious to the individual concerned, but the investigator needs a conceptual framework to make the patterns of rules stand out from the background of social action. These patterns, which are based upon social action or performance, can be discovered by 'ethogenic' methods. The objectives of these methods are to discover what people know about these rules (their social resources or *competency* to perform) and what use they make of this knowledge to bring into play the appropriate behaviour to pursue their goals (their *performance*).

Harré's approach is descriptive rather than quantitative. But this is a point of departure rather than a final methodology. By looking at the nature of rules using a particular conceptual analogy of social exchange (see particularly Roloff, 1981, for a summary of social exchange theories) it is possible to explain the rules of performance as a system of exchange of resources, where a score is kept. Cohen and Bradford (1989) describe influence within an organization as connected to an ability to negotiate and to exchange valued resources. These resources become organizational 'currencies', are mainly intangible, but are potentially scoreable. Coonradt (1985) has developed a training system based on the analogy of exchange and score-keeping.

To measure the impact of structure or *context* on management performance we need to:

- understand the different types of structural systems operating within an organization, and be able to distinguish between either discrete systems or between different points on a continuum;
- understand the underlying rules operating within these systems – how they apply to management roles – and determine individual managers' understanding of these rules, and their application of them in their performance;
- compare a measure of structural system, and application of rules, with a measure of management performance and results.

A structuralist approach, therefore, concentrates on the context of performance and its prevailing influence on what people actually do: the goals they aim for, and how they achieve them. This is further taken up in Chapter 6.

Phenomenology

This term is mainly drawn from social philosophy (eg Schutz, 1972), and has been developed as a sociological theory (eg Berger and Luckmann, 1966, and Cicourel, 1964). It also has origins in psychological theory (Goffman, 1959) and has been developed as an approach to psychotherapy and psychology in client-centred, humanistic or existential approaches to therapy (Rogers, 1951), in attribution theories (Kelley, 1967 and 1973) and personal construct theory (Kelly, 1955), as well as in other psychological theories. Much of this is consolidated by Silverman (1970) in his book *The Theory of Organizations* by what he calls the 'action' frame of reference. This perspective contains the following assumptions:

- *Action* is the subject of interest rather than *behaviour*.
- Action arises from *meanings*.
- Meanings are individuals' definitions of social reality.
- They arise from our interactions with society, become formal-

ized and are handed down as social facts to succeeding generations.

- These social facts are also interpreted by the individual, but are reinforced by continual reaffirmation in every-day actions.
- Interacting individuals modify, change and transform these social meanings.
- Explanations of human action (eg management performance) must take account of these meanings which individuals assign to their actions.

A phenomenological approach is therefore concerned with the meanings of our actions (actions are types of behaviour which have meaning) or the interpretation of a social situation of the individuals concerned. It sees the social environment as a product of meaning negotiated between interacting individuals, and therefore approaches human performance from the opposite direction to structuralism.

We give meaning to our social world through our perceptions: perceptions of self (how we see and value ourselves – self-concept), perceptions of others (person perception), and the meanings we attribute to events, particularly how we explain cause and effect (attribution).

Self-concept is the way we see our own abilities to perform in the roles we occupy. We can summarize its nature, its construction, and its importance to management performance as follows (see also Jackson, 1984:139):

- self-concept is a self-percept: the way we see ourselves.
- It is both descriptive and evaluative: what Argyle (1967) calls 'self-image' and 'self-esteem' respectively.
- Self-concept is an internalized social construct arising through social interaction within a particular social setting and cultural environment (Mead, 1934).
- Since it arises through social interaction, it is dependent on our role occupancy during that interaction and our perceptions of our enactment of that role (Goffman, 1959).
- The self-concept affects the social interaction in which we are involved as we see ourselves, as we believe others see us (Cooley's, 1902, 'looking-glass self'). So, not only do we arrive at these beliefs about ourselves by interacting with others, we actually interact with them according to these beliefs.
- It is essentially an attitude. Contained within attitudes is a predisposition to respond to a social situation in some way: to act (Burns, 1979).

Person perception ('social perception', McArthur and Baron, 1983, or 'interpersonal perception', Cline, 1964) is the way we see and judge other people in a social situation: their moods, intentions, personality and thoughts. This is dependent on:

- the perceiver's own self-concept and their prior experience, and the way they categorize and conceptualize their world;
- the social situation in which the perception occurs (Forgas, Argyle and Ginsberg, 1981);
- what it is about the other person which is being perceived or judged (Cook, 1988).

People act towards other people according to the way they see them rather than the way they actually are. Distortions may occur through stereotyping and other prejudices, but quite simply, different people may see the same person in completely different ways.

Individuals will see another person according to their own frame of reference (see Kelly, 1955, for example). However, psychologists also use particular frames of reference for looking at other people, and these, after all, are just other ways of perceiving people! The question may be asked, are these psychological frames of reference any more valid than common-sense perceptions of other people?

Psychologists construct analogies of reality, frames of reference, for example in personality theory where people are categorized as 'extroverted' or 'neurotic' (Eysenck, 1970). These categories are not necessarily the reality itself despite what some psychologists believe! These analogies may help us to categorize and to better understand other people's intentions and actions, and may help us to compare one individual with another.

However, before attempting to construct these frameworks within which to perceive other people, we must understand the common-sense constructs: how managers see and understand those other people they work with, and how this affects the way they interact with them. We should not forget, though, that psychologists may actually influence common-sense thinking through the popular media, and the introvert/extrovert dichotomy is a good example of this.

As well as making judgements about other people, individuals also attempt to explain events and outcomes in terms of cause and effect. *Attribution* theory has developed to try to explain the way people attribute cause and effect to events and to people's success or failure, particularly in terms of internal and external causes (see Lalljee, 1988).

Managers may attribute success or failure in their jobs to either their own behaviour, what they did or did not do (internal control), or to luck or problems within the organization which are beyond their control (external control), or a combination of the two (for example, the facilities or opportunities were not available to them to receive the necessary training to properly perform the job, although they could have taken better advantage of the opportunities that were available).

Rotter (1966) has developed an internal-external (I–E) scale to measure an individual's position on this 'locus of control' dimension in general terms. That is, individuals can be divided into those who tend to give 'internal' explanations and those who tend to give 'external' ones. However, I–E explanations given by individuals depend on their own self-regard and the circumstance. For example, when student teachers were asked to explain the performance of their pupils, they attributed failure to the child and success to their own teaching methods (Johnson, Feigenbaum and Weiby, 1964). Miller and Ross (1975) describe these effects as 'self-protection' and 'self-enhancement'. Other studies have tended to minimize these 'motivational' effects.

Kelley (1967, 1973) suggests that people use 'co-variation' information, referring to variables of persons (consensus), entities (distinctiveness) and time (consistency). An example will help to clarify this. A manager may judge that a job is difficult to perform if most people who do that job find it difficult (consensus). If Jill finds the job difficult, does she also find other jobs difficult? If not, it may be that particular job is more difficult than the others she has done (distinctiveness), particularly if other people find that job difficult (consensus).

Does Jill always find this job difficult, or just sometimes (consistency)? Where most people find the job difficult (high consensus), where Jill finds other jobs easy (high distinctiveness) and always finds the job difficult (high consistency), the outcome will be attributed to the entity (that particular job) rather than to the particular attributes of Jill.

To measure the impact of personal meaning systems or content on management performance we need to:

- understand how managers see themselves – their self concepts;
- understand how managers see others with whom they work – their social perceptions;
- understand how managers explain events, such as people's performance or their own career progression – causal attribution;
- understand how this impacts on action and specifically man-

agement performance, including the comparison of measures of content with measures of management performance and results.

A phenomenological approach, therefore, concentrates on the meanings that individuals negotiate with others through interacting with them. An example of a consolidation of approaches to this is Kelly's (1955) personal construct theory which looks at the ways people form constructs to predict and to control their environment. This theory is capable of taking into consideration the three facts discussed above: self concept, person perception and attribution. Kelly's methodology can be used to learn a great deal of the way perceptions may affect performance, and it also overlaps onto personality and motivational theories which we will return to later (see pp. 95–8).

Behaviourism

This term is used here to denote those psychological theories which centre around the importance of observable behaviour. In the extreme, behaviourism sees overt behaviour as the only means of explaining the psychology of a person: behaviour as a response to stimuli in the environment, and not a result of an inner cause. Although 'inner states' are accepted, they are not deemed relevant to a scientific explanation of behaviour in Skinnerian terms (Skinner, 1953).

We are not concerned here with pure behaviourism, save to note the origins of this approach. The emphasis on skills, from more contemporary psychologists, is a descendent of behaviourism, and is relevant to an understanding of management performance.

Particularly relevant is the work of Argyle (for example, 1967) and colleagues (for example, Argyle, Furnham and Graham, 1981), on social skills. The approaches of Morgan (1979) and Rackham, Honey and Colbert *et al* (1971) also represent the behaviourist/skills tradition. Rather than behaviour being the beginning and end of behaviourist interest, in social skills theory the 'skilled performance' is the end product of both internal and external processes. Argyle's (1967) skills model shows the skilled performance as emanating from both the objectives of the work being undertaken and the internal motivations of the performer.

The social skills approach can be regarded as reductionist in the sense that it is studying something by taking it apart (Singleton, 1980), by focusing on the elements of human performance. Singleton points to the difficulty of doing this with complex social processes which are interconnected in an intricate way. To put this into perspective it is worth returning to our Criteria 1: 'To be useful a science must discover what would otherwise be hidden', and to Harré, Clarke and De Carlo's (1985) level 1 to level 3 hierarchy (p. 26).

Level 3, deep structure/social order we have addressed, albeit implicitly by looking briefly at structuralism. We have addressed level 2, conscious awareness by looking at phenomenology. Behaviourism/skills addresses level 3 by focusing on behavioural routines. There is no reason why we should not discover 'what would otherwise be hidden' by focusing on the minutiae of social life, or management performance, any less than focusing on the 'higher order' controlling factors of social order of society or organizations.

Indeed, it is a central theme throughout this text, that by making apparent the nature and influence of these three levels of analysis we can influence management performance at the behaviour end of this hierarchy.

We have already alluded to the distinction between 'action' and 'behaviour', and we should here define exactly what we are interested in, focusing on the behavioural end of the hierarchy.

Behaviour could be simply a physical movement or emitted sound which can be described without referring to the culture or intention of the person concerned. Behaviour may sometimes 'just happen', but usually it is intended. This is an *action*. It is not simply a behaviour, but without reference to the culture concerned we are not able to distinguish it as an *act*. An act only has meaning within a culture (Harré, Clarke and De Carlo, 1985).

To simply begin by looking at human actions, in much the same way that a social anthropologist might study a lost tribe without a clue as to what their actions mean, we would have to start with the smallest elements of behaviour, how they are strung together, and finally what they mean to the actor and co-actors.

It is difficult to describe a human behaviour without reference to its social meaning. It is difficult to understand that meaning without reference to the explanation of the actors (see Silverman, 1970, and Harré, Clarke and De Carlo, 1985). It is equally difficult to explain action simply by reference to the observable performance, and not to the competencies or resources required of the performer. We must ask, what is the body of knowledge and wherewithall needed to carry out certain activities, and how is this body of knowledge put to use? (Harré, Clarke and De Carlo, 1985).

Our area of interest is therefore in skilled *performance*, which comprises *acts*, which have meaning for the individual managers concerned and the organization. To be a skilled performer the manager requires certain *competencies*, resources, or knowledge to be able to perform successfully. Success is measured against recognized *standards* of achievement which can be referenced to laid down *criteria* or *norms* of the wider management group. Often these can be related to actual results.

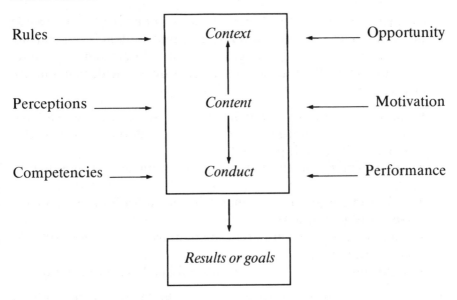

Figure 2.5 *Accessibility of information in the context–content–conduct, model*

Generally speaking those factors on the right of Figure 2.5 are in some ways accessible information available to us by observing or inferring on the basis of what we can see or what might be public knowledge, and what might be the basis of common sense. Usually, by a systematic study of these factors, we can improve on common sense; we might regard this approach as the basis of positivist methodology discussed in Chapter 1. Thus:

- Opportunity may simply refer to the organizational arrangements, types of jobs available and the career structure within an organization. Lack of opportunity may be an explanation given to poor motivation.
- Motivation may be inferred from enthusiasm for work and demonstrated by speed of work, volume of work, and prepared-

ness to take work home and so on. Lack of motivation may be given as an explanation of poor performance.

- Performance is observable and may be compared with what is usually expected of a manager occupying a particular role. It may be judged by reference to achievement of results or goals: poor performance may be given as an explanation for poor results, as might lack of motivation or lack of opportunities to adequately perform.

Those factors on the left of Figure 2.2 may not be readily accessible by observation or inference, and it is here that content is our starting point: we must *communicate* to get the information. Communicating involves obtaining the information we require by the design and use of instruments which:

- discover information which otherwise would not be available to us and the managers concerned (see criterion 1:) for criteria 1–6, see Chapter 1, pp.26–31;
- are acceptable to the manager's common-sense (see criterion 2);
- offer something to the manager in return for honest responses (see criteria 3 and 4);
- transcend or make apparent the manager's prejudice and bias (see criterion 5);
- yield information which can be validated (see criterion 6).

We may also discover information about the factors on the right of the Figure 2.5 by using similar methods, and alternative methods of enquiry may serve as corroboration.

At the end of the day, what matters is that we are able to construct an adequate analogy of the reality of management performance; that is, it complies with our six criteria.

Let us summarize the place of communication within our model of the three Cs: context, content, and conduct. Communication is comprised of these three components:

In this chapter we have taken the criteria for a scientific study of management performance developed in Chapter 1, and have looked at an analytical structure which incorporates the ideas of context, content and conduct, with communication as a central theme. We have explored the theoretical basis of these three ideas and have brought them together into a general framework for looking at management performance.

Component	Description	Easy to access	Difficult to access
Context	The structure and rules which have an impact on our communication	'Opportunities' observable through *conduct*	'Rules' accessible only through *content*, by finding out people's perceptions
Content	Own thoughts and ideas about a situation, others and self, some of which are communicated	'Motivation' is inferable by observing behaviour, ie through *conduct*	'Perceptions' accessible only through asking questions and revealing information about own thoughts and attitudes, ie others' *content*
Conduct	Skills and behaviour of an act of communication	'Performance' can be observed through *conduct*	The 'competencies' needed to perform well cannot be accessed directly. Access requires an understanding of *content*

Figure 2.6 *Communication and the three Cs*

We will now look more specifically at this framework and how it can be used in the measurement of performance.

3 Measurement and Management

In the concluding chapter of this Section we look more specifically at the nature of measurement. Firstly we look at the social characteristics of measurement as both information and presentation, and its role as feedback within an organizational setting. There is evidence to suggest that through some sort of measurement of performance feedback is effective in enhancing performance, although reservations are expressed here about too much 'external' feedback within a learning situation.

By using measurement as feedback we intervene in the communication process and this is taken up next. Particularly applicable is the use of performance ratings given by others and self awarded. Where there is a disparity between raters it may mean that organizational communication is poor: that is there is little sharing of ideas on perceptions of a manager's performance. We may therefore use the feedback of measurement data to enlighten the manager about such communication problems who may then need to ask the question: why do my colleagues not have the same view as me?

However, things are not quite as simple as this. We have to consider the problems of reliability and validity of measurement instruments. If we get these basic aspects of effective measurement wrong then we cannot expect to use inter-rater disagreement on a manager's performance as indication of a problem with communication. The section 'Making measurement effective' therefore goes into some detail.

This section is important if the reader is to construct his or her own measurement instruments, but can be skimmed over otherwise.

Finally, the practicalities of designing a measurement instrument are discussed in this chapter. A step-by-step approach is provided for those readers who wish to design a measurement questionnaire.

MEASUREMENT AS FEEDBACK

As well as exploring the uses and means of measuring management performance, contained within this text is a major hypothesis which has implications for the way measurement is seen and used by those who seek to develop managers. This hypothesis is based on a view of human science which includes rather than excludes the 'man in the street'. It is based on a view that theory is useful to management practice, that a successful science of management performance is one which contributes to the success of managers in their workplace. It is based on a perspective of a science as *facilitating*: helping management move forward.

The view put forward here is that measurement is an analogy of reality (performance); which can be fed back to managers to change their perceptions and therefore to change their performance. This stems from a distinction, developed in Chapter Two, between measurement as *information* and measurement as *presentation*. Measurement can intervene in the communication processes of an organization by impacting on both our perceptions and possibly our actions, within an already existing pattern of perceptions which individuals might have about relations within the organization. Let us consider this a bit more clearly.

If we measure a manager's performance this can provide certain information about how that manager performs. However, the measures taken have not simply an informational value. The purpose of measuring, the use made of the information, and the way that information is 'presented' all mean something to the person being measured, and have implications for the organization.

A manager may feel under threat from senior management if his or her performance is being measured (particularly if this implies being checked on, or being appraised for a salary review or bonus), or may feel that the measurement is helping (for example as part of a development tool or training needs analysis as is seen in McEnery and McEnery, 1987). The organizational climate and management styles of senior management, as well as other factors, may contribute to perceptions and reactions of managers along the following dimension:

Being judged   Being supported
|_____|

In fact this is also a criterion for perceiving individual measures of performance as well as a complete measurement process. Another dimension along which perceptions may be made of a measurement process is the extent to which the manager being measured perceives having control over the use being made of the measures, as follows:

Can affect this measure		Cannot affect this measure

Again, this may also be a criterion for perceiving the value of an individual measure.

Although it is difficult to separate the two functions, we can summarize the distinction between measurement as information and measurement as presentation in Figure 3.1.

Returning to the view that measurement can be used as feedback to improve performance, this has support in the research literature and is fairly well documented in learning theories. McCormick and Ilgen (1985) suggest that feedback on behaviour serves two purposes in the learning process: a *directional* function, giving information to the learner necessary to perform the job (information on what is being done right and what is being done wrong); and a *motivational* function, giving information about the outcomes of a performance which may be associated with rewards (intrinsic rewards such as satisfaction, or external rewards such as pay awards).

Pritchard and Jones *et al* (1989) have developed a specific method of productivity measurement aimed at increasing employee motivation through feedback of measurement information, facilitating goal setting, and enabling a common focus on specific goals. They recorded productivity increases of 50 per cent across five units during feedback sessions in a study undertaken within the US Airforce.

Komaki, Heinzmann and Lawson (1980) undertook a study of training with and without feedback over a 45 week period with vehicle mechanics, and found that where training was conducted with feedback there was a significant improvement in performance from training where feedback was not built in.

There seems little doubt that feedback with training improves training results, and there is some evidence to suggest that feedback alone increases performance. However, the exact nature of the motivational function of feedback is unclear and questions remain. Ilgen, Fisher and Taylor (1979) discuss the possible factors which influence the effectiveness of feedback as a motivator. These can be the credibility of the source of feedback, frequency and timing of the feedback, whether the feedback is positive or negative (with positive feedback being more effective), the specificity of the feedback (feedback relating to specific aspects of performance is more effective than general feedback), the relevance of the feedback to goals being pur-

Measurement as:		
	Information	**Presentation**
Characteristics	Serves only to provide information such as feedback or comparison of one case with another	Serves a perceived purpose which may carry a threat or a reward
	Has no value judgement	May have a value judgement, and may be seen along a continuum of being judged/being supported
		Has a social meaning.
		May have 'political' connotations
Purpose	Usually only for scientific research where no connection is made with the organization, and no benefit is seen by the person being measured	For organizational purposes, which are known to the person being measured or are assumed to be known
	Note: no measurement has purely an informative purpose, as perhaps the classic Hawthorne study shows (summarized in Brown, 1954)	Social impact varies depending on organizational purpose, eg annual appraisal, training needs analysis

Figure 3.1 *Measurement as information and presentation*

sued, and the individual psychological differences of the individuals receiving feedback.

Feedback can also be either internal or external. Ribeaux and Poppleton (1978) refer to this as 'intrinsic' or 'augmented' feedback, where the former is connected directly to the individuals performance through perceptual cues, the latter is any source external to the person receiving feedback. Sometimes used synonymously with these criteria are 'knowledge of performance' and 'knowledge of results'. The former is concerned with *concurrent* feedback, the latter concerned with *terminal* feedback. Miller (1953) suggests that where there is consistent and frequent use of external concurrent feedback, the learner may use this as a crutch, rather than using the concurrent intrinsic feedback information relied upon once out of the learning situation.

However, Holding (1965) contends that where insufficient external feedback is given during a learning process – which would provide external standards of performance – learners tend to rely on intrinsic feedback and develop their own performance standards.

These two appraisals can be summarized as follows.

Feedback:		
	Internal	**External**
Descriptions	Intrinsic	Augmented
	Knowledge of performance	Knowledge of results
Timing	Concurrent	Terminal
Disadvantages	No external standards or criteria of performance	May be used as a crutch instead of developing own stndards and checks on performance
Advantages	Develops own standards and checks on performance	Provides standard-ization of performance
Appropriate	Outside the performance learning situation where the individual is responsible for own work	In the learning situation where standards are being set; and where assessment of performance is required

Figure 3.2 *Internal and external feedback*

This debate indicates that there is still a great deal to learn about the motivational and learning implications of feedback. It is particularly relevant to the focus of this text: the provision of specific performance information used as systematic feedback to managers to develop their performance.

Another key issue regarding measurement as feedback is the question of the source of measurement: who measures? This question brings us neatly back to the theme of communication.

MEASUREMENT AND COMMUNICATION

We have already said that a central core in management activity is communication. At the risk of stating the obvious, to perform effectively managers need to communicate since this is how they relate to those with whom they work. In order to measure management performance we need to consider this key factor and accommodate it within a measurement strategy. Before explaining this further let us first define communication in context as this will help to clarify:

> Communication is the process whereby individuals' internalized social experiences are shared by the establishing of relationships between two or more persons within a community and whereby attitudes or behaviour are modified and through which social experience is created. (Jackson, 1984)

This definition of communication is central to the social psychological approach taken to measurement in this text, and will be developed in more detail in Chapter 9. We can aid the process described above, which is so vital to management performance, by facilitating a sharing of 'internalized social experiences' and in so doing can change attitudes and behaviour.

Let us suppose that we ask managers to rate themselves on various management activities, and then ask the people they work with (peers, subordinates, superiors) to rate them on the same activities. If there is wide disparity in the ratings, could we not conclude that something is amiss? Although a manager may think he or she is a good manager, the people around that manager might not share the same opinion. Could this mean that the manager is falling down on the key process of managing, ie communication (a sharing of internalized experience)? Could we facilitate a sharing experience by making the disparities apparent?

Wohlers and London (1989) undertook a study of ratings of management characteristics – self-rated and rated by co-workers – and compared the differences between self-, superior, subordinate and peer ratings with four 'self protection' factors of 'denial', 'giving up', 'self-promotion' and 'fear of failure'. They found that there was a stong correlation between managers using self denial (that is a lack of self-awareness) and evident disparity between self- and co-workers' ratings.

This study is interesting since it goes half way to making some sort of connection between management communication (a sharing of experience) and accuracy and agreement of performance ratings. People become self aware through effective communication with others. In Mead's (1934) terms this is seeing your self as others see you. The other conclusion which Wohlers and London (1989) make is that regarding ratings of characteristics which are open to interpretation and are difficult to rate, there is greater disparity between self- and co-worker ratings, as perhaps would be expected. Again this is a function of communication where the rating factors themselves are not good communication.

MEASUREMENT STRATEGY

In summary, the questions we will need to answer will therefore be:

- Specifically, what information can we gain through measurement methods about managers' performance, which can then be fed back to improve performance?
- From which sources do we obtain this information, and in the case of performance ratings, who do we ask to rate the manager?
- How can this feedback be used to facilitate improvements in management performance?
- How can we tell if by feeding back this information management performance has improved?

We can adopt the following strategy, building on the theories discussed in this Chapter. Our strategy is, figuratively, to hold a *mirror* up to the performer in order to facilitate communication, develop self awareness, and aid self-development. Graphically this can be represented as in Figure 3.3.

This approach has certain implications for the way in which management competency and performance can be viewed, and would bear out Jacobs' (1989) remarks, for example, that management competences for adequate performance are not necessarily universal as

Mirror (communication)

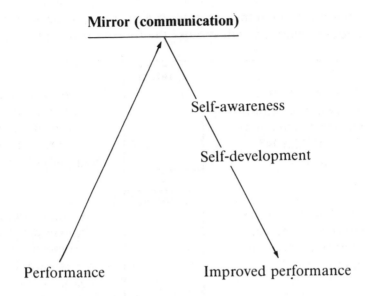

Self-awareness

Self-development

Performance   Improved performance

Figure 3.3   *Feedback on a mirror*

the Management Charter Initiative in the UK suggests. Management is a social activity and relies on the make-up of the social units within which management, as a process, takes place.

We must first clarify what it is which makes a manager effective within the social situation he or she is in. This involves looking at the *context* of performance (the rules of the game within the particular organizational and social environment), the *content* of that performance (perceptions and expectations of the manager and co-workers), and *conduct* (the actual process of management with resultant products or results).

For each manager, in each social situation, the reflection in the mirror may be different. The *process* of clarifying the reflection may be the same. This process will be drawn from our theory and scientific methods. It is not absolutely essential that the practising manager understands all the nuances of these methods for this theory to comply with the criteria of a science which we discussed earlier. What the manager will need to understand clearly is the *reflection in the mirror*, which will clarify his or her perception to such an extent that, starting from common sense but transcending prejudice and bias, it: will provide information that the manager would not otherwise have; will change or modify perceptions, allowing the attainment of results they would not otherwise have produced; and will be capable of verification (see criteria 1 – 65, pp. 24–32).

A template of communication as a mirroring process follows, and subsequent chapters will discuss the process involved.

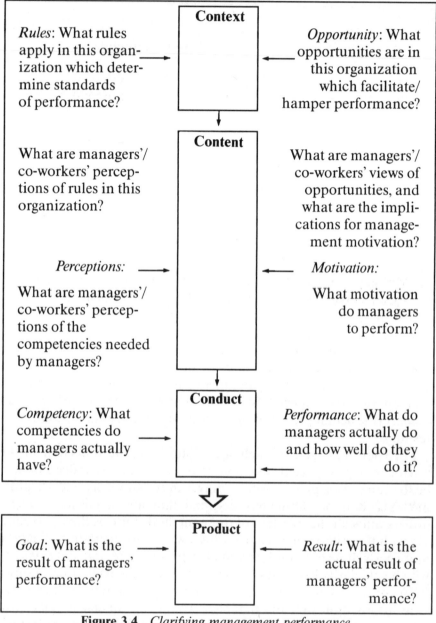

Figure 3.4 *Clarifying management performance*

To summarize, a framework based on a view of science and the relation between theory and management practice has been constructed to provide a mirror, which can be held up to the practising manager to clarify those areas affecting his or her performance. Factors affecting actual performance are categorized under the broad headings of context, content and conduct. Content is seen as a central core from which we can, starting from common-sense ideas, begin to get a picture of how factors under the two other headings can impact management performance.

A basic process is outlined (pp. 57–58) for using the mirror approach and this will be developed in subsequent pages, as will specific instruments and methods which can be used to extract the information needed to construct the mirror.

MAKING MEASUREMENT EFFECTIVE

In this chapter we have looked at the use of measurement as feedback in a developmental process, and have begun to develop ideas about measurement as communication (more fully developed in Chapter 9). Before proceeding to investigate further specific measures of management performance in Section Two, we must look at some general considerations of measurement theory and practice to enable us later to develop more effectively specific measures of aspects of performance. These considerations are covered extensively in a number of standard works on measurement and assessment (eg Anastasi, 1988; Cronbach, 1984; Aiken, 1988; Kline, 1986).

Any measurement method in accepted psychometric theory should yield both reliable and valid results. *Reliability* and *validity* have specific meanings. A test or measurement instrument is said to be reliable if it is internally self consistent, and if it gives the same score on two separate test occasions for the same subject (Kline, 1986). Essentially, a test or measurement instrument is reliable if it is relatively free from unsystematic errors of measurement (Aiken, 1988). If it consistently measures under varying conditions that can produce errors then the test can be said to be reliable. Aiken (1988) points out that systematic or constant errors may inflate or deflate test scores. As long as they do so in a constant manner they do not render the test unreliable.

In classical theory of measurement error it is assumed that for any characteristic on which an individual is measured, he or she has a 'true' score. Any test will be composed of this true score plus unsystematic error. The true score is the average of the scores that would be obtained if the individual took the test an infinite number of times. In reality this can never be obtained, and the true score must be estimated from the actual scores on the test taken. If taken a number of times there should be a normal distribution of scores around the mean score (the mean approximating the true score). The standard deviation of the error distribution around the mean is an index of error.

The classical theory of measurement error also assumes that the true score of an individual would be obtained if he or she were given all items (eg questions in a questionnaire) from the 'universe' of items relevant to the characteristic being measured (eg intelligence). In most cases of course, this universe of items is hypothetical and therefore classical theory assumes a test comprises a random sample of items from such a universe.

The average correlation of one test with all possible tests in the universe which measures the particular characteristic, is the reliability coefficient. As this cannot be obtained in practice, the reliability of a test is only an estimate and any statistical index of reliability can only be regarded as an estimate, indicated as r_{11}.

There are three main methods of estimating reliability suggested in the literature (eg Rust and Golombok, 1989; Aiken, 1988; Kline, 1986), only one of which is really practical in a busy management situation. The three methods are test-retest, parallel forms and split-half.

The first two methods are considered by this author as largely unworkable unless the subjects are extremely patient and tolerant! An example of these methods is the type of measurement instrument which allows managers and co-workers to assess performance of the manager (further elaborated in Chapters 8 and 9). It is often quite difficult to persuade managers and their co-workers to participate in this type of testing, and the tester must show that there is something in it for the participant; for example, that it will aid their self-development and they will receive detailed feedback on the results of the tests. In this example there is a direct pay-off for the managers – the subjects of the study – but not so for the co-workers. There is therefore a need to get the test 'right first time' in the eyes of the co-workers, since they are unlikely to co-operate as easily again. A test-retest to establish test reliability is not feasible! However, a split-half test is, although this is generally regarded as somewhat of a compromise in the literature.

Let us first look briefly at these methods to see how we can best establish reliability in a practical management situation.

Reliability is the measure of accuracy of a questionnaire or test. If a manager obtains a similar score on the same test on different occasions – provided he or she has not changed in any way which affects the score – then the test can be assumed to be reliable. Test-retest requires the same questionnaire to be administered to the same individuals on two separate occasions under similar circumstances. Where there is a high correlation (ie 0.7 and above) between the two separate scores, then the test is assumed to be reliable.

Apart from the problem of co-operation discussed above, this method suffers from the difficulty of achieving similar circumstances and ensuring that subjects have not developed at all since the previous test. If you give managers feedback on performance this may lead to further awareness and further development simply as a result of the feedback involved. Furthermore, there is a problem of gaining the same level of attention and motivation on the second.test. Rust and Golombok (1989) also suggest that subjects may also remember responses to the first questionnaire, and therefore the parallel forms method may be appropriate where two similar questionnaires are constructed using different items from the universe of items available to test the particular characteristic. Here it may be difficult to select two equivalent sets of items.

For practical reasons the current author favours the split-half method where the questionnaire is essentially divided in half between similar items which purport to test the same characteristic, and to obtain a correlation between these two halves.

The correlation coefficient can be calculated using the Pearson product-moment formula see Cohen and Holliday, 1982). Rust and Golombok (1989) suggest the use of the Spearman-Brown formula to give an estimate of questionnaire reliability as follows:

$$r_{11} = \frac{2r_{1/2\ 1/2}}{1 + r_{1/2\ 1/2}}$$

Where: r_{11} = estimated reliability of the questionnaire
$r_{1/2\ 1/2}$ = correlation between the two halves

The classical theory of measurement error – an important consideration in conceptualizing reliability – reinforces the view of measurement as an analogy of reality discussed above (p.27). The abstract nature of the true score – that is, one which can never be obtained –

suggests that we can never exactly reproduce reality through measurement. We are only going to gain an insight or an approximation of that reality. However, the idea of true score acts as a standard (albeit theoretical) towards which to work.

Before proceeding to discuss validity, it is worth looking at two concepts related to internal reliability: 'facility' and 'discrimination' of test items within a questionnaire, a check on which can be made when investigating split-half reliability. These concepts, discussed in Rust and Golombok (1989), concern the effectiveness of the items in a questionnaire.

Questionnaires are usually designed to distinguish between respondents on the basis of the particular characteristic being measured. For example, to distinguish between less or more intelligent people. If all individuals taking the test respond to an item in exactly the same way, that item does not help in differentiating between respondents for that particular characteristic. Facility is an indication of the extent to which individuals respond to an item in the same way. If an item is facile it is useless to the questionnaire and must be discarded. The facility index is calculated by dividing the number of respondents who give a particular response to the item by the total number of respondents (this should fall between 0.25 and 0.75, giving an average of 0.5 for the questionnaire).

Discrimination is the test's ability to discriminate between respondents on the characteristics being measured by the test. Items should only be left in a questionnaire if they correlate well with other items measuring the same characteristic. Rust and Golombok (1989) suggest a minimum correlation of 0.2, usually choosing 70–80 per cent of the original items and rejecting those items with a zero or negative correlation.

The best way to perform an item analysis along the lines suggested above is through constructing a correlation matrix; that is, correlating each item with every other item. This technique is explained in the literature (Rust and Golombok, 1989; Aiken, 1988) and is best performed using a computer programme such as SPSS (a useful, inexpensive and much simplified package is MYSTAT: see Bibliography).

Reliability is regarded as a prerequisite for validity. A test is valid if it measures what it claims to measure. Each aspect of validity contributes to an overall demonstration of validity as follows.

Face validity is important as a prerequisite to test validity. If managers think a test is irrelevant, stupid or sloppily presented this may affect their attitudes towards completing it. This aspect is extremely important when dealing with busy managers. If you do not get this right, then the overall validity of the test may be affected.

Whether or not the stimulus material in the test measures the entire domain or universe of the characteristic, skill, understanding or behaviour that the test is supposed to be measuring is a matter of *content validity*. This must be established through developing criteria specific to the test involved. In the case of a selection test, its content can be compared to the job specification to determine whether it includes and represents those aspects of the job which it purports to measure. The test specification must match the task specification; that is, it must cover what it says it is covering. If it covers other attributes or characteristics not relevant to the task, then it must be testing something other than what it says it is testing.

Concurrent validity can be established by correlating the results of the test with results of other tests which purport to test the same thing. This may be relatively easy in, for example, intelligence testing where there are many established tests. However, the question arises that if there are other tests against which a new test can be validated, what is the point of a new test? In the case where there are no other similar tests, it may be difficult to establish concurrent validity. This type of validation has little importance without reference to the other forms of validity.

Construct validity (Cronbach and Meehl, 1955) requires the delineation of the construct or variable which the test is attempting to measure. By doing so it is possible to overcome some of the problems of concurrent validity where a new test is being constructed in order to measure theoretical ideas which are somewhat different to existing ideas. Such an example is the conceptual-intuitive manager construct which is fully described in Chapters 8 and 9. We can say, for example, that intuitive managers manage 'by the seat of their pants', are likely to be more results-oriented than their conceptual colleagues, more pragmatic and less willing to complete questionnaires. On this basis we can establish certain hypotheses about the intuitive manager which correlate highly with action/pragmatic learning styles in the Honey and Mumford 'learning styles inventory' (Honey and Mumford 1982) and which are more prevalent in fast-moving, sales-oriented organizational cultures. We could then test these hypotheses in order to establish construct validity.

Predictive validity may be established by correlating scores on a test with some later criterion such as job success. The difficulty is in selecting an appropriate criterion for success, and generally predictive validity is only useful for aptitude, ability or intelligence tests.

Once a measurement device is validated, it is appropriate to establish norms for scores on the test over a larger population. The reason being that a score of 37 on a test may mean nothing unless related to the normal distribution of scores over the population (eg all managers) as a whole. For example, an IQ score of 100 is meaningful as it represents an average score for intelligence over the whole population (ignoring arguments for and against IQ testing as an appropriate measure of intelligence). Norms are usually presented in terms of mean and standard deviation for each specific group of individuals (eg sales managers, personnel managers).

The nature of different types of test which purport to measure various characteristics relating to management performance will be discussed in Section Two of this text.

In this Chapter we have looked at various aspects of measurement: first at the use of measurement as feedback; then at measurement as communication, going on to fit this into a general strategy for measurement; and then looking at considerations for providing effectiveness in measurement, drawing on classical theory of measurement error.

One of the methods not mentioned above, and used to provide a validation of a test instrument, is obtaining correlations between ratings of managers' performance by the managers themselves and those of their co-workers. Generally, if similar results are obtained then this can indicate the degree of *convergent validity*, where the results from all different parties are pointing in the same direction. This is a form of *triangulation* (eg Cohen and Manion, 1980) which attempts to give a view of a subject from different angles. This method using multiple raters is also used to counter the effects of rating error, which principally occurs through leniency, halo, bias or range restriction (see Tsui and Ohlott, 1988, and McEnery and McEnery, 1987 for example). Self-ratings tend to be more lenient than co-workers' ratings (McEnery and McEnery, 1987). Halo occurs when raters allow an overall impression to influence their ratings on individual characteristics, thus not distinguishing between the different aspects of a test. Bias is simply defined as a lack of correlation between self-ratings and ratings of others. Research is not consistent in this area (McEnery and McEnery, 1987), but well-defined constructs and well-designed questionnaires are regarded as a prerequisite to freedom from bias. Range restriction is where ratings cluster around a narrow section of a rating continuum – the tendency to go to the central point on the scale for example, or the unwillingness to rate anyone negatively, or to use the extremes of the scale. Superiors' ratings have been shown to exhibit the greatest tendency towards range restriction (see Tsui and Ohlott, 1988).

It is proposed by the present author that differences in perception recorded by co-raters on the performance of the subject manager, in addition to the problems discussed above, are problems of communication within the organizational unit concerned. Indeed, Tsui and Ohlott (1988) suggest that differences in perception and information processing are a source of disagreement among raters observing the same ratee ('cognitive' models of performance ratings). This has led to reports of higher agreement among raters at the same organizational level (ie peers) than between raters at different organizational levels.

Processing of the information concerned involves:

* observation;
* forming a cognitive representation of behaviour;
* storing the representation in memory;
* retrieving it for evaluation;
* reconsidering and integrating the retrieved information with present information;
* assigning the formal evaluation.

Therefore information recalled and acted upon in a test or evaluation may differ widely across the individual raters (see Tsui and Ohlott, 1988, for a review of studies undertaken in this area).

In addition, different raters may use entirely different criteria upon which to judge a good performance, and this may affect results between raters.

However, it is argued here that the source of error in these examples is the degree of effectiveness (or lack of it) of communication within the organizational unit. The better the communication the more agreement there will be between co-raters. Indeed, it is possible to use this agreement level as the basis for an index of effective communication.

We will be returning to these issues in Section Three after we have considered the different measures of management performance in Section Two. First we will apply some of the principles of good measurement, to constructing a measurement instrument.

METHOD: DEVELOPING A TEST

Rust and Golombok (1989) describe a method for developing a test which we outline here.

Step 1. Identify the purpose of the test. This should be stated as it is important that we have a clear idea of what it is we are testing for. This should ideally be based on theory or a model of performance.

Step 2. Identify the content areas of the questionnaire. What is the content area of your questionnaire? You may want to test good communication or a particular style of management for example. Write down the things you wish to test for.

Step 3. Identify the manifestations of these content areas. How do we know when these content areas are manifested by the subjects in question? How do they demonstrate good communication, or a particular style of management? For example, this may be through the way they make decisions, or relate to others, or relate to the work tasks.

Step 4. Construct a grid with 'content areas' at the top, and 'manifestations' at the side.

Content areas

Manifestations	*High performance*	*Low performance*
Demonstration of skills		
Demonstration of motivation		
Results achieved		

Step 5. Write the items for the questionnaire. In each cell of the grid, items can be written which correspond to the content area, as manifested by the description: for example an item written for 'high performance' manifested by a demonstration of skills. Suitable items might be 'has finely tuned management skills'. As many items as necessary should be written in each cell, allowing for some which you

may reject. A decision about the total number of items for the questionnaire must be made. A minimum of 20 is usually required as a requisite to reliability, but more should be added (up to 50 per cent more) for those items which may be rejected after the pilot. Select equal numbers of items from each cell in the grid ready for your pilot, unless you wish to assign different weights to each content area and each manifestation.

As part of step 5 you must also make a decision about the type of item you wish to include in your questionnaire. The options are as follows.

- Alternate choice: answering 'yes' or 'no', 'true' or 'false' for example.
- Multiple choice: giving more than two choices of responses, consisting of a stem, eg a statement followed by four or five option responses. With a knowledge test one option is correct, the others are distracters.
- Rating scale: where the response is along a continuum such as 'yes', 'don't know', 'no', usually up to seven options being used. Alternatively, numbers on a continuous scale may be used to indicate a strength of feeling, attitude or even performance. It is desirable to explain what the numbers mean, for example 5 = feel very strongly, 1 = don't really care.

Step 6. Design the questionnaire. Good design is important to face validity discussed above. It should incorporate:

- Background details of the questionnaire, why it is important for the respondent to complete the questionnaire, and what will be the benefits to this person: the questionnaire must be sold at this stage.
- Instructions must be clear and straight forward, on the assumption that the subject-manager is going to be busy and possibly impatient. Say clearly how the subject must answer the questions or respond to the items.
- Personal information such as name, age, sex, length of time in service, job title and so on may be required.
- Layout of the questionnaire should be simple and attractive, looking inviting to the respondent. Number each item and keep it short. At the top response items or scale remind the respondent again how they should be completed (eg 'tick as appropriate'). The response items themselves should be in a straight vertical line on the right hand side of the page. Above all, experiment with the design until you get it right: small, closely-set type looks

rather formal; larger type well spaced out on a warm-coloured paper looks friendlier.

Step 7. Pilot the questionnaire. Use a small sample of subjects similar to those you will use in the main study. These may be a cross-section of managers in the organization if you intend eventually to test all managers. As a 'rule of thumb' the minimum number of respondents for the pilot should be one more than the total number of items in the questionnaire.

Step 8. Conduct an item analyis. This should test for facility and discrimination. Draw a grid with each column representing an item, and each row representing a respondent. If your questionnaire consists of knowledge-based items, in each cell place a 0 for a wrong answer and a 1 for a correct answer; if person-based items, write into each cell the actual score. Sum the scores for each cell to give a total for each row (each respondent), and total score for each column (each item).

If every respondent gives the same answer to an item, this does not differentiate between different respondents and therefore has poor facility: these items are therefore redundant. A facility index should be calculated in the following two ways.

For knowledge based items: divide the number of respondents obtaining the correct response for an item by the total number of respondents. A facility index less than 0.25 shows the item is too dificult and over 0.75 shows it is too easy. The index should therefore be between these amounts and average 0.5 for the whole questionnaire.

For person-based items: divide the total sum scores for the item for each respondent by the total number of respondents. An index which equals or approaches the extreme scores for each item indicates that the particular item must be dropped from the final questionnaire. But make sure that if the facility index lies in the middle of the extreme score, this does not indicate extensive use of the middle score by respondents.

Discrimination is the degree to which items measure the same knowledge or characteristic as the other items of the questionnaire. Clearly, if respondents who do well on a questionnaire consistently get the wrong answer for one item, then that item may not be measuring the same content.

To measure discrimination each item must be correlated with the total score of the questionnaire. The higher the correlation the more discriminating the item. A minimum correlation is regarded as 0.2, and generally 70–80 per cent of the original items are selected for the final version of the questionnaire. Items with a zero or negative correlation are excluded. The Pearson product-moment correlation (see Cohen and Holliday, 1982) is normally used, correlating the score for each respondent for an item with the total score for each respondent for the questionnaire. This can be done by hand using the method described by Rust and Golombok (1989), but is more commonly calculated by computer (see the references for MYSTAT and SPSS in the Bibliography).

Once you have conducted this analysis you can select your items for the final version of the questionnaire.

Step 9. Calculate the reliability of the test. Reliability is a measure of the questionnaire's accuracy, and a questionnaire is reliable, for example, if a respondent achieves a similar score on separate occasions. We have recommended that in most management situations a split-half method is used, employing the Spearman-Brown formula (outlined on p. 61). Following this method, items should be selected from the pilot questionnaire which collect parallel information, producing two sets of items. The correlation between these two sets over the sample – which should be as large as possible (ideally about 200) – should be at least 0.7 for person-based, and 0.8 for knowledge-based questionnaires.

Step 10. Calculate validity. Validity is the extent to which the test measures what it says it measures. We have above (p. 62–64) looked at the different types of validity. Face validity is a prerequisite of course, and content validity is taken care of in the item analysis. Read through the information on different types of validity to determine which types of validity are important to the particular test being designed, using the Pearson product-moment correlation formula to calculate the correlation coefficient.

Step 11. Standardize the test. Where it is necessary to compare scores of individuals with groups of the population, for example all managers or all production managers, it is desirable to produce norms for the test over a large number of respondents. Norms should be presented in terms of the mean and standard deviation for each group. This can be calculated on most scientific calculators, or by hand, referring to any statistical textbook, if a computer programme is not available.

In this chapter we have considered the use of measurement, how to make measurement effective, and how to apply this in test construction. We now turn to existing methods of measuring different aspects of management performance (competencies, culture and styles, motiation) and their underlying theories.

SECTION TWO

MEASURING MANAGEMENT PROCESS AND RESULTS

Whatever exists, exists in some quantity and can
(in principle) be measured. (E L Thorndike)

INTRODUCTION

We turn now to the existing practice of management performance measurement and find ourselves in the thick of the competencies debate. In some ways we side-step this debate by using the word 'competency' rather than the predominant 'competence', defined by the UK Training Agency as 'the ability to perform the activities within an occupational area to levels of performance expected in employment' (see the Training Agency report: *Management Challenge for the 1990s*, July 1989). Our idea of competencies is built up throughout this section.

We start by looking at the role of management – what managers actually do – and then go on to look intensively at competencies, and to evaluate the current debate. By means of illustrating some of the pitfalls we examine leadership as a competency, first looking at the theory of leadership and seeing how this relates to more practical considerations.

Always with an eye on the three major factors of context, content and conduct, we look more specifically at the rules of management by focusing on culture and on a major aspect of performance, motivation.

Measurement as feedback and as a development tool is used as a focus throughout.

4 The Nature of Management Performance

We will call the results of a manager's performance, where these contribute to the business which the organization is in, his or her *products*. These may be 'tangible' or 'intangible', but in any event can be subject to some sort of quantification or measurement which makes comparison between managers possible over time. Both tangible and intangible products can be quantified by use of an analogy, but the more intangible the products the more abstract becomes the analogy, and the more complex the analogy is to construct, the more difficult it becomes to get agreement on the analogy used.

To recapitulate the discussion in Section One, any measurement is an analogy or representation of reality. It is not the reality itself. Hence we represent time by numbers on a clock face, and we represent temperature by numbers on a scale on a thermometer.

Thus we can represent products by the number of units produced in a factory (tangible or 'hard' products) or, for example, by the value which a manager adds to the human resources in his or her charge, as represented, for example, by utility analysis (intangible or 'soft' products) (see Chapter 5). The latter is an analogy which is far more difficult to construct and one which does not easily obtain management commitment as a measure of performance and relevant to the management situation.

We have already mentioned (pp. 55–56) the difficulty of getting agreement on ratings which are open to disagreement (Wohlers and London, 1989). This, plus the difficulty in constructing an analogy and obtaining agreement on it provides two dimensions which should be considered when obtaining product measures.

Difficult	Easy to
to measure	measure

Difficult to	Easy to
obtain	obtain
agreement on	agreement on

It is difficult to obtain direct, hard products for managers, and therefore the literature has tended to concentrate on competencies (and sometimes actual performance) rather than the products of performance. This really leaves two options: either obtain measures of hard products obtained indirectly as a result of managers' performances; or construct an analogy to obtain measures of soft products obtained directly (or indirectly) as a result of managers' performance.

Before we proceed on these problems we should first clarify what it is that managers do, what managers achieve, and then go on to see how we can represent (analogically) these achievements?

What a manager is, is not something on which there is common agreement. This, perhaps, is one of the most difficult problems of measuring management performance. Everybody thinks they know what a manager is! We can all point to someone in an organization and say 'that person is my manager!', but does that mean the same thing in one organization as it does in another? More particularly, in an age of multinational organizations, is a manager in Japan the same as a manager in the USA or in Sweden?

Is it possible to single out particular roles, aspects or attributes which all managers have which identify a person under any condition and any culture as a manager? These problems of definition will be addressed in this chapter.

WHAT IS A MANAGER?

Managers have different job descriptions, with different actual duties, and thus different emphases on the managerial parts of their work and the technical or non-managerial aspects of their work. To define what a manager is, is to perhaps define what he or she does. But different managers do different things! Is it not possible to point to a definition of management which covers all managers so that we can say 'this person is a manager' or 'this person is not a manager'?

Much has been written on management activities, competencies and skills, and much money is spent on educating managers through MBA (Master of Business Administration) and other management programmes. There is little evidence in the literature, however, of an adequate definition of what management is other than by referring to management activities and competencies. There is also disagreement about what a manager's role is, and if there is a general function of management (for example in Herriot, 1988).

Our task here then, is to offer a definition which will include some jobs but will exclude others; that will not label everyone as a manager simply because they carry out certain managerial functions. A tentative working definition is as follows.

A manager is someone whose main responsibility is to organize other people's time within an organization, in order to pursue the objectives of the organization, and whose primary activity is in communicating with others to achieve these ends.

The adequacy of this definition we will review against the accepted view of management roles, activities and competencies.

MANAGEMENT ROLES

The main problem in trying to define what a manager is, is that there are different levels of management with different types of role. Torrington and Weightman (1985) provide one categorization as follows:

Top managers: relatively detached from organization; few in number but with very important responsibilities; spend most of their time with outsiders and with peers, very little with subordinates.

Senior managers: head of function or operation; concerned with policy formulation and implementation; work tends to be hectic and frequently interrupted; often out of office; spend time dealing with outsiders, peers and subordinates.

Middle managers: work mainly within the organization and are concerned with making the organization work; can be line or staff; work mainly with peers and senior managers; calmer situation than that of senior or supervisory managers.

Supervisory managers: relatively detached from management hierarchy and concerned with the day-to-day activities of the organization; busy, frequently interrupted and constantly switching between jobs; spend most time with subordinates, some time with peers and little with superiors or outsiders.

Mintzberg (1973) undertook a major study in North America into what managers actually do at the various levels of management, and concluded that there are certain common elements (around the basic function of communicator) which are applicable to all managers in varying degrees depending on their particular role within the organization. He identifies eight types of managerial jobs to which he refers as follows:

- The contact man: figurehead and liaison with outside.

- The political manager: outside the organization trying to reconcile conflicting forces that affect the organization.
- The entrepreneur: seeks opportunities and implements change in the organization.
- The real-time manager: builds up and maintains stable systems over time.
- The insider: tries to build up and maintain internal stability through resource allocation.
- The team manager: preoccupied with creating a team which operates effectively as a cohesive whole.
- The expert manager: advises other managers and is consulted on specialized problems in addition to other managerial duties.
- The new manager: so far lacks the contacts and information to be any of the above.

Mintzberg (1973), who sees a manager's pivotal function as communicator, then identifies specific roles of managers. These roles are reflected to a greater or lesser extent in different management jobs outlined, and can be categorized as follows:

The interpersonal roles of:

- Figurehead: a symbolic role.
- Leader: motivating subordinates, staffing and training.
- Liaison: maintaining network of contacts.

The informational roles of:

- Monitor: receiving information regarding the organizational environment.
- Disseminator: interprets and transmits information to subordinates.
- Spokesman: provides interpreted information about organization to outsiders.

The decisional roles of:

- Entrepreneur: finding opportunities and initiating projects to effect change.
- Disturbance handler: taking corrective actions when problems occur.
- Resource allocator: making decisions to allocate resources.
- Negotiator: representing the organization in major negotiations.

Stewart (1976), undertaking similar research in the UK, took a different approach by seeing managers as essentially different and having different functions depending on their particular job. Stewart also sees managers as: either a *hub* with contacts, subordinates, superiors, peers, and others above, below and on the same level; *peer dependent* with less vertical demands and more emphasis on co-operation with peers, and often found on the boundaries of an organization; *man-management* concerned with vertical relations; or *solo*, working alone on assignments.

Stewart (1985) later develops this, categorizing different types of managerial jobs as follows:

- Emissary: represents the organization to the outside world, spending little time in the office.
- Writer: dealing with information processing, usually in specialized functions and with a limited amount of contact with other managers.
- Discusser: with a range of responsibilities, spending a great deal of time with other managers.
- Trouble shooter: dealing with crises as they occur, the job is largely unpredictable, with large amounts of time being spent with subordinates.
- Committee member: concerned mainly with decision making in formal group-based discussion, typically working in large organizations and having little contact with the outside world.

The above categorizations emphasize the differences in management functions by focusing on different roles. What about the similarities? How can we identify a manager other than by his or her title?

MANAGEMENT ACTIVITIES

Mintzberg (1973) identifies six basic purposes of managers, or reasons why organizations need managers:

1. To ensure the organization serves its basic purpose in producing specific goods or services.
2. To design and maintain the stability of the organization's operations.
3. To direct the organization's strategy and adapt the organization, in a controlled way, to environmental changes.

4. To ensure the organization serves the ends of those who control it.
5. To provide an information link between the organization and its environment.
6. To operate the organization's status system, as its formal authority.

This categorization is perhaps the most helpful in validating our earlier definition of a manager, since it emphasizes management activities by focusing on the objectives of the management function.

Generic management activities have also be identified, for example:

(Miner, 1978)

- planning;
- organizing;
- supervising;
- co-ordinating;
- communicating;
- controlling;
- investigating;
- evaluating;
- decision making;
- staffing;
- representing;
- bargaining/negotiating.

(Mullins and Aldrich, 1988)
Fundamental activities

- clarifying goals and objectives;
- planning;
- organizing;
- motivating and developing staff;
- measuring performance.

Substantive activities

- communicating;
- co-ordinating;
- integrating;
- having responsibility;
- making decisions.

(Campbell *et al*, 1970)

- handling administrative details;
- supervising personnel;
- planning and direct action;
- acceptance of organizational responsibility;
- acceptance of personal responsibility;
- proficiency in speciality.

Campbell's classification relates directly to research undertaken in the US Airforce, but is interesting since it also provides principal activities which are not exclusive to managers: handling administrative details, acceptance of personal responsibility, and proficiency in speciality (the latter stated by Campbell as 'proficiency in military occupational speciality').

The position taken in this text is that although managers are often required to be technical specialists (this is how they have probably become managers by being good at their previous job which required a technical expertise, rather than through their managerial ability!) when they are pursuing their own technical or professional activities they are not managing. Managers achieve results through others. Their technical expertise may enable them to make good managerial decisions and to control the work, but as managers, when they achieve a result directly associated with their own profession – as a result of solo activity – they are no longer managing.

THE CROSS-CULTURAL ISSUES

One of the fundamental problems with getting agreement on the nature of management performance is the diversity of management cultures. This is also of relevance when looking at only one country since different types of industry harbour different types of attitudes and ideas about what constitutes a manager, and moreover what constitutes a good manager.

In a small customer-oriented company there may only be one manager who fulfils all the roles of Mintzberg's or Stewart's classifications. On the other hand, in a large office-based organization, many people may hold the title of manager but may also be doing different things, having only a part-time responsibility for managing other people, with the vast bulk of the job being taken up with specialist or technical responsibilities.

When we start to look at the role of the manager internationally, we may come up with different approaches and different ideas about what a manager is. Certainly we will derive different criteria for measuring management performance. From this we can take two different approaches.

1. Management, internationally, is basically the same: managers simply achieve results through organizing the time of others in accordance with the objectives of the organization. The manager who operates on an international basis should therefore be able to adapt to different cultures but still obtain results through others (see definition on p.76) .

2. Management is essentially different in different cultures and we cannot really compare one manager in one culture with that in another (whether it is in the same country in different organ-

izations or in different countries). Each organization should therefore have the wherewithall to develop its own criteria for good management and hold its own views on what a manager should do and how thcy should perform.

The first of these approaches is implicit within the Management Charter Initiative in the UK, where attempts are being made to develop generic management competencies applicable across organizational cultures. The second of these is perhaps reflected in the approaches of companies developing their own lists of competencies within the UK, and this is fully discussed in Chapter Five.

The present text tries to accommodate both these views but suggests that these approaches might be inadequate for the problem of measuring management performance, even if they provide a good start in doing so.

More pertinent to the cross-cultural measurement of managerial performance is the assessment and understanding of the contribution of the three management sub-systems referred to in Chapter Three, namely: deep structure (level three), conscious awareness (level 2), and behaviour routines (level 1). These sub-systems are also referred to under context-content-conduct in Chapter Two and developed as a template for measuring management performance in Chapter Three. Essentially, this template outlines an approach which requires the collection of the following information:

1. What are the rules which apply in the organization, which determine standards of performance?
2. What are the perceptions of managers and co-workers regarding these rules and what are their perceptions of the competencies managers require to comply with these rules?
3. What are the competencies managers have?
4. What are the desired and actual results of managers?

We will explore these aspects of management performance throughout Section Two, starting with a view of management competencies, and then developing a specific approach to management performance measurement in Section Three.

METHODS FOR ANALYSING MANAGEMENT JOBS

A straightforward method for analysing jobs is used as part of the management analysis questionnaire described later in this text, and can be used as follows.

Ask managers to complete the following.

To give an idea of what your job entails, please allocate your time between the activities below. For each activity circle the appropriate percentage.

Circle appropriate %

1. Technical/professional
   activities concerned
   with your specialization   10 20 30 40 50 60 70 80 90 100
2. Selling/promoting/PR   10 20 30 40 50 60 70 80 90 100
3. Planning   10 20 30 40 50 60 70 80 90 100
4. Implementing decisions   10 20 30 40 50 60 70 80 90 100
5. Developing staff   10 20 30 40 50 60 70 80 90 100
6. Controlling/co-ordinating   10 20 30 40 50 60 70 80 90 100
7. Troubleshooting/problem-solving 10 20 30 40 50 60 70 80 90 100
8. Rewarding performance   10 20 30 40 50 60 70 80 90 100
9. Obtaining direct results   10 20 30 40 50 60 70 80 90 100
10. Other (please specify)
    ....   10 20 30 40 50 60 70 80 90 100

Total should add up to 100%

Briefly describe the objectives of your job.

....

....

....

....

This information can be used to look at the percentage of time spent actually managing, and differences between functions and between levels of management.

Another technique which can be used is that derived from Reddin (1989) which compares a manager's effectiveness areas with his or her authority areas (see also Chapter 5.) on the basis that managers should not be held accountable for results in areas for which they have no authority (and cannot control output). This will give a clear analysis of the jobs which all managers do in the organization and the compatability between what they are expected to achieve and what they have authority to decide.

Simply get managers (and their superiors) to write a job analysis as follows.

Write down those areas for which you are accountable; that is, the outcomes which you are expected to deliver.

In my job I am accountable for ....

Now write down your authority areas; that is, those areas in which you can make decisions.

I can decide on ....

----

5 Competencies and Results

MANAGEMENT COMPETENCIES

Management activities are also a basis for defining management competencies. So following Miner (1978) for example (see Chapter 4), we can list competencies such as:

- is able to *plan* work;
- is able to *organize* the work of others;
- is able to *supervize* others' work etc.

We can define competencies as a manager's 'inner resources': a capability to do something.

Much of the classic management literature fails to take account of the changing nature of management work and its position within a commercial enterprize. Perhaps this is because the 'classicists' did a lot of research work into administration type jobs, and Campbell *et al* (1970) (see Chapter 4) is a case in point.

It is worth looking at some of the modern, 'popular' literature on management competencies which takes account of new demands on managers. Greatrex and Phillips (1989) looks at the competency assessment system in British Petroleum, which has generated the following clusters of management competencies:

Achievement orientation
- personal drive;
- organizational drive;
- impact;
- communication.

People orientation
- awareness of others;
- team management;
- persuasiveness.

Judgement
- analytical power;
- strategic thinking;
- commercial judgement.

Situational flexibility
- adaptive orientation.

The above reflects a more positive commercial bias as regards what managers are expected to do and expected to know.

Cadbury-Schweppes' categorization of managers' competencies is related by Glaze (1989) as follows.

Strategy
- vision;
- critical thinking;
- innovation;
- environmental awareness;
- business sense.

Drive
- self-motivation;
- initiative;
- tenacity;
- energy;
- independence;
- risk taking;
- resilience.

Relationships
- sociability;
- impact;
- acceptability;
- awareness.

Persuasion
- oral communication;
- written communication;
- flexibility;
- negotiation.

Leadership
- delegation;
- subordinate development.

Followership
- followership;
- teamwork.

Analysis
- problem analysis;
- numerical analysis;
- listening;

- creativity;
- judgement;
- intuition.

Implementation
- planning and organizing;
- decisiveness;
- organizing sensitivity;
- management control;
- work standards;
- detail handling;
- compliance;
- stress tolerance;
- adaptability;
- commitment.

Personal factors
- integrity;
- management identification;
- career ambition;
- learning ability;
- technical/professional.

These two company lists of competencies not only reflect what managers do, but also what is expected of managers within the respective organizations: what is highly rewarded and what is not. Above all, they list the types of behaviour and attitudes which are appropriate for the particular organizations. Of course what is acceptable as a list of management competencies in a public corporation or civil service department may not be wholly acceptable in a commercial organization. For example, note the difference in emphasis between Campbell *et al* (1970) and Greaterex and Phillips (1989) above. Other competency categorizations include:

1. Manchester Airport plc (Jackson, 1989):

Understanding what needs to be done
- critical reasoning;
- strategic vision;
- business know-how.

Getting the job done
- achievement drive;
- proactivity;

- confidence;
- control;
- flexibility;
- concern for effectiveness;
- direction.

Taking people with you
- motivation;
- interpersonal skills;
- concern for impact;
- persuasion;
- influence.

2. National Westminster Bank (Cockerill, 1989):

- information search (to make decision);
- concept formation (on basis of information);
- concept flexibility (consideration of alternatives);
- interpersonal search (understanding others ideas and feelings);
- managing interaction (team building);
- developmental orientation (creating a developmental climate);
- impact (to gain support for ideas and initiatives);
- self-confidence (confidence for implementing own ideas);
- presentation (communicating ideas);
- proactive orientation (implementation);
- achievement orientation (ambitious yet attainable goals).

Focusing on a generic approach, Dulewicz (1989) looks at 'supra' competencies, or those competencies required of a high-performing manager. Information is obtained by self- and superior-assessment of high-flying middle-managers at Henley, The Management College, on 40 specific competencies. From these competencies are derived 12 performance factors as follows (adapted from Dulewicz, 1989):

Intellectual
- strategy and perspective;
- analysis and judgement;
- planning and organizing.

Interpersonal
- managing staff;
- persuasiveness;
- assertiveness and decisiveness;
- interpersonal sensitivity;
- oral communication.

Adaptability
- adaptability and resilience.

Results-orientation
- energy and initiative;
- achievement motivation;
- business sense.

Dulewizc (1989) also notes the similarities between the list of supra competencies produced at Henley and those competencies lists used in practice in the companies referred to in the same series of articles in *Personnel Management* (Greaterex and Phillips, 1989; Glaze, 1989; Jackson, 1989; Cockerill, 1989). Indeed, apart from some reformulations of terminology and perhaps a more specific business-orientation of some of the competencies listed in the literature and in company appraisal forms, it is difficult to see what the new spate of interest in management competencies adds to the work of the 'classicists'. We can summarize this as follows.

To be effective a manager needs to be able to:

Motivate him/herself and others
- achievement orientation (BP, NatWest);
- drive (Cadbury-Schweppes);
- taking people with you (Manchester Airport plc).

Make appropriate decisions
- information search (NatWest);
- concept formation/flexibility (NatWest);
- judgement (BP);
- strategy (Cadbury-Schweppes).

Communicate
- impact (NatWest);
- interpersonal search (NatWest);
- people-orientation (BP);
- relationships (Cadbury-Schweppes).

Be adaptable and developmental
- development-orientation (NatWest);
- situational flexibility (BP).

Achieve results
- implementation (Cadbury-Schweppes);
- getting job done (Manchester Airport plc);
- proactive-orientation (NatWest).

The above is not exhaustive. Other company classification systems can be found in Jacobs (1989) for example, and some competencies classifications such as 'leadership' (eg Cadbury-Schweppes' classification including 'delegation' and 'subordinate development') might span motivation, decision making, communication and adaptability, resulting in our classification above. However, we treat 'leadership' as a special case below, since it is often used synonymously with 'management'.

Where factor analysis has been used in organizational research (see Herriot, 1988), similar groupings of competencies are derived from specific competencies correlating well with each other, and reflect similar broad headings as our classification above. Perhaps the exception is that of 'administrative skills' which features in at least eight studies undertaken between 1969-79. However all these studies quoted by Herriot (1988) are of an age when administrative skills may well have been emphasized (even used synonymously with 'management skills') in contrast with the business orientation currently emphasized in many organizations and in the literature.

The point here is that either the topical debate in the UK (and in the US) on management competencies does not really add much to our understanding of what good managers do (we already know that good managers communicate well and that they make good decisions, for example) or it adds to the debate by emphasizing particular aspects of management competencies which are important in some organizations and not in others.

A useful way of looking at this is through the concept of 'skills language' developed by the Institute of Manpower Studies (IMS) at the University of Sussex (Hirsh, 1989, and Hirsh and Bevan, 1988). This approach focuses on the language companies use to describe what makes a good manager. Hirsh (1989) outlines the problems as follows:

'Although there is almost a "national prototype manager" in terms of some very common expressions of "skills", we cannot infer that these terms have common meaning in different organizations. (p.11)' Indeed, she focuses on 'leadership' as having the most diverse interpretation, which tends to be a personal characteristic in graduate selection of managers but a skill when appraising existing managers. 'Decision-making' in one company researched by Hirsh (1989) meant taking 'innovative decisions', and in another meant 'analysing hard data and minimizing commercial risk' (p.12).

In order to clarify the language of management skills in specific organizations, Hirsh (1989) suggests using a three-level 'hierarchical list' as follows. For example, if an organization develops a first-level categorization of 'personal factors' (as does Cadbury-Schwepps), a second-level factor might be 'integrity'. The third level would be a description of what integrity actually means in the organization. This third-level description could usefully be written in behavioural terms: that is, how is this attribute or characteristic manifested in what the manager does; or what can potential management recruits actually demonstrate to show they have this attribute?

Hirsh (1989) goes on to describe the two methods used in organizations to derive this 'skills language'. These are:

1. *Brainstorming*. This usually involves personnel and management development specialists in an organization getting together to generate and react to lists of words and expressions about management skills, drawing on their experience of management performance in the organization. Usually this method generates lists of personal attributes and is often influenced by latest fashions and thinking in management competencies, depending on what the personnel specialist has read no doubt!

2. *Internal research*. Often involving outside consultants, internal research can be undertaken by interviews and questionnaires. Interview methods can focus on 'critical incidents' in the recent experience of the managers interviewed and can focus on the attributes of managers who are seen as particularly successful. Co-workers of managers can also be useful sources of information. Psychometric tests are also used in internal research to try to single out attributes of current successful managers, which can then be identified in recruits and potential managers. This type of research can highlight current differences between functions in an organization, but it does tend to dwell on current requirements for the job rather than the future needs and demands of the organization and the work of the managers.

There are two ways round this problem of focusing on current rather than future needs, one of which is pointed out in Hirsh (1989). That is, to focus more on generic lists of attributes of high potential managers which correlate strongly with high performance in most management jobs. This is certainly the approach of Dulewicz (1989) mentioned above, who has produced a generic hierarchical list of supra competencies. The interested reader is referred to this list.

The other approach which can be useful, in a period of organizational change when managers are not sufficiently developed for the future to comment intelligently about their future roles, is to take a developmental approach. It is often difficult for a practising manager to see past the immediate demands of the job. A developmental programme which seeks to educate managers into thinking about future needs and about their own strengths and weaknesses can immediately precede an information-gathering exercise, which puts managers into a better position to view the future. The only problem with this approach is that comments regarding attributes of the 'future manager' are often repeats of specific concepts managers have learnt on the programme and are not directly generated by the circumstances of their organization's strategic needs.

The research conducted by the IMS (Hirsh and Bevan, 1988, and Hirsh, 1989) points to various aspects of good practice in deriving skills language in the 40 organizations involved. These can be summarized as follows:

- Short and simple lists are easier to use.
- Specialist and functional skills should be taken into account.
- Skills language may be a pragmatic mixture of tasks, activities, knowledge, personal attributes, skills and competencies.
- Skills descriptions should be written in behavioural terms where possible.
- Methods for deriving skills should be rigorous and subject to validation.
- Skills lists should focus on the future as well as on the present.
- Skills language should be 'harmonized' across levels of management and across functions.

The latter is an important point since it recognizes that not all managers do the same thing, although what they do may be related to more generic functions and skills. An example provided by Hirsh (1989) is the difference in three levels of management – supervisor, departmental manager and executive director – where the supervisor 'supervizes others', and the departmental manager and executive director 'manage people'. Similarly, the supervisor 'interacts with others', the departmental manager 'interacts with other departments' and the executive director 'represents' the company. These three levels of management are reflected in the language used to describe the same basic skills.

The first item in the points of good practice above, 'short and simple lists', is important from a concept-handling perspective. The more complex, the more difficult a skills list is to use. However, from the

IMS study (Hirsh and Bevan, 1988) a list of some 5–10 main headings was normal in the 40 companies investigated. This restriction in variety, the authors suggest, leads to an apparent similarity of skills between organizations. This may be far from the reality, where interpretation of the same words and phrases used may be quite different.

Finally, the question one must ask of this research into skills language – particularly as a large proportion of skills derivation is undertaken by outside consultants or internal personnel specialists – is how much is the language used that of the organization itself, reflecting the culture of the organization, and how much is the language used that of consultants or the literature imposed on the organization? Forty-eight per cent of the skills documents examined in the IMS study was derived by the personnel function, and 15 per cent resulted from external constultant's input. Only 13 per cent was derived from input from managers themselves. To be fair however, multiple sources were often used in the organization researched, combining informal input from managers with the views of the personnel function.

The 'natural' language of managerial skills requirements may differ considerably from one organizational culture to another. The imposition of 'textbook solutions' to the problem of skills identification may be a mistake if the solution is wrong for the culture. In later chapters we identify specific cultural contexts which impact on the skills language and methodologies used, and we draw this together in Section Three of this text.

The conclusion drawn so far is that the basic skills or competencies of management may be similar across different organizational cultures. For example, all managers need to be able to communicate well to be successful. However, the language of skills is essentially an analogy or a code for what managers actually do or need (see the discussion in Section One of this text). As such, across organizational cultures the same symbols (language) may mean different things in different organizational contexts. These codification systems have to be analysed to derive the specific concepts and meanings behind the language (whether the language is 'textbook' or whether it is the 'natural' language of the organization).

The astute reader will have noticed that the terms 'skills' and 'competencies' have been used almost synonymously, particularly by Hirsh (1989), in the above discussion. 'Competencies' usually refers to all embracing characteristics and attributes of managers in terms of their 'inner resources' from which they can draw; 'skills' are more behaviourally based and are directly demonstrable through action.

To a large extent, in every-day usage in organizations these two terms are interchangeable.

We will now discuss what can be done to derive skills and competencies language.

METHODS FOR DERIVING SKILLS LANGUAGE

There is a number of uses for skills language in organizations, including selection, performance appraisal, assessing future performance for promotion purposes, and training needs analysis. It is important that all the functions within an organization concerned with these various aspects (they do not always lie within the same department) agree on the language used. Agreement must be sought from personnel specialists, line managers and senior management on the skills language used and its meanings and applications to the various levels and functions of management. The following approaches are suggested.

1. Existing documentation. If appraisal documents exist which list attributes of successful managers, these should be used as a starting point. Ask the questions:

- How old is this documentation?
- It is still relevant to the needs of the organization?
- How is it regarded by line managers? Cynically? Do they use it carefully as an appraisal document?

2. The help of senior management. Where possible, bring together a group of senior managers to discuss:

- The relevance of existing documentation.
- The changing needs of the organization.
- The attributes they would look for in a successful manager, with an eye to the future.
- What attributes have helped the senior managers themselves to be successful in the organization, and if these attributes are still relevant.

A hierarchical structure for documenting senior managers' responses can be used to probe deeper. For example, interpersonal skills may be mentioned as a prerequisite for managerial success. Could they explain in a bit more detail what this means and what it entails. This may elicit responses along the lines of being 'personable', 'articulate', 'a good communicator' or 'has an understanding of people and able to empathize'. So what do they mean by these phrases? Could they point to specific behaviour examples of managers using these skills? This may then give rise to the following responses regarding interpersonal skills, for example:

- *Personable*: Is able to relate well with people from different backgrounds, to mix well at formal and informal social occasions, and can quickly develop a relationship with others. Others respond openly and warmly to this approach.
- *Articulate*: Is able to present a good case orally in formal situations, be persuasive and engender a positive response from others.
- *Empathetic*: Demonstrates an understanding of other people by dealing with them tactfully and sensitively, eliciting openness and loyalty from others.

As a hierarchical list is compiled there may be some overlap. For example, there is some overlap between 'personable' and 'empathetic' in the partial list above. This can be looked at again after the next stage in the process of deriving skills language.

3. *Obtain structured information from the line.* It is important to try to find out the 'natural' language of skills used by practising line managers (and where appropriate from their co-workers) in order to 'get beneath the culture' of the organization. This is a valuable aid to tuning any subsequent skills list to the culture, making sure that it is acceptable to the culture and is not at variance to it. Personal construct theory (Kelly, 1955) is a theoretical framework for looking at the way people conceptualize their world, and the ideas they have of such issues as good management. Repertory Grid is a method used to elicit people's personal constructs in a systematic way, and this method has been used successfully in obtaining information about the language of skills in organizations. We therefore suggest this method is used in the following way in order to obtain a feel for the 'natural language' and prevailing ideas of management performance. Draw up a grid as outlined in Figure 5.1.

This grid can then be used either in a one-to-one interview or in a group session with a selection of managers from the organization. They should be asked to write in the names of six managers at the head of the columns 1–6 in the following order. Columns 1 and 2 should be managers they know or have known who are regarded as being highly effective and the type of managers required by the organization in the future. Columns 3 and 4 should be fairly effective managers within the confines of the immediate job, and 5 and 6 should be not very effective managers they know.

	1	2	3	4	5	6	7 Self	8 Ideal self		
									Name	**Date**
									Construct	**Contrast**
1	•	•	•							
2			•	•	•					
3	•					•	•			
4		•		•			•			
5			•		•		•			
6	•			•			•			
7		•			•		•			
9		•				•	•			
10	•			•	•					
11										
12										
13										
14									*Effective manager:* the future of the organization	*Ineffective manager:* in the organization today
15										

Figure 5.1 *The Repertory Grid*

Taking a row at a time, they should then compare the three managers indicated by the dots in each row. They should also be asked to compare themselves and their ideal selves (columns 7 and 8) with these managers as indicated by the dots in each row. For each comparison, they should select some aspect related to management effectiveness which makes two of the three people being compared different to the third. This attribute or characteristic should be written under the heading 'construct' and that attributed to the third person should be written under 'contrast'.

For each row, once they have produced a construct and contrast they should rank each of the eight persons (these are called 'elements' in Kelly's 1955, terminology) 8 to 1, giving 8 to the one who possesses the construct the most, and 1 to the one who possesses it the least (usually possessing the contrast the most, although the contrast is not necessarily a direct opposite of the construct). They should rank all others along this scale, and not give any equal ranking.

Finally, in the final row, rank all persons (8–1) against the construct 'effective manager: the future of this organization', and the contrast 'ineffective manager in the organization today'.

The grid should then be analysed. In the row immediately following the ranking for the final construct/contrast, reverse the rankings given in the final row. The construct which the subject managers have created can now be compared with the general measures for 'effective manager' in the final row as follows.

Example

Row 3	0 1 7	0 1 5	2 3 1	1 5 2	0 4 1	0 8 7	0 7 5	3 6 0	6 28R
Final row	1	2	5	6	4	8	7	3	
Reversed row	8	7	4	3	5	1	2	6	

Figure 5.2 *Analysis of the Reportory Grid*

The top row is an example of one of the construct rows, the second row the general effectiveness score, and the bottom row is the effectiveness score reversed. In the top row, the middle figures are the original rankings. The top figures are the difference between the specific constructs and the rankings on the general effectiveness row. The bottom figures are the difference between the specific construct ranking and the general effectiveness score reversed. The total for the differences are added and shown at the side of the row.

If the total reverse score difference is smaller than the total for the effectiveness score difference, then the construct is reversed with the contrast (eg in our example above, 28R is larger than 6, therefore the construct remains the same).

We now have a direct comparison (a crude correlation) between the construct of 'effective manager: the future of the organization' and the individual constructs. The lower the difference score, the higher the relationship between the construct and effectiveness in the view of the subject manager. The constructs can now be listed in rank order of effectiveness.

A comparison can now be made of the constructs of all subject managers to derive those features or attributes of managers which are seen as being important to management effectiveness (particularly with a view to the future). From each manager's grid take the five constructs which correlate closest to the effectiveness construct. This should provide a good spread of competencies. Any constructs which are similar can be combined, to give a list of those attributes of good management as perceived by the practising managers within the organization.

The language used may well reflect popular literature in this area, or may be quite superficial. For example, the present author obtained such attributes as 'lucky' as a management competency from one source. The implications of this for management styles and organizational styles will be fully discussed in Section Three of this text.

4. Synthesis. More information about the meanings of individual manager's constructs may be obtained through personal interviews using the hierarchical structure suggested in approach 3 above. Once this information has been obtained, it is time for the personnel specialists within the organization to structure the information by compiling a hierarchical list, across function and across management level, which reflects the views expressed. The lists of competencies given in this chapter may help, as will the sources already quoted. However, the finished list is a matter of judgement exercised by the human resources function and it is difficult to describe in this volume how to acquire such judgement, although by following the methods described, enough insight should have been gained enabling a finished article to be produced.

LEADERSHIP: AN EXAMPLE OF
A MANAGEMENT COMPETENCY

'Leadership' is often assumed to be almost interchangeable with 'management'. It certainly features highly in skills and competencies lists as we have pointed out earlier. However, we can assume that leadership and management are different things, and that leadership may mean different things in different organizations. There is no doubt that this aspect of management is an important one since it transports the idea of management as a passive 'supervisory' role, where subordinates are simply influenced to fulfil the minimum requirements of their jobs, to actively encourage others to participate fully in achieving the objectives of the group (see for example McCormick and Ilgen, 1985). This idea is certainly reflected in the skills list of Cadbury- Schweppes (as reported by Jacobs, 1989):

- *Leadership*. Getting the best out of subordinates individually and collectively, achieving objectives in the most effective way.

and in W H Smith Ltd (Jacobs, 1989)

- *Leadership*. Shows skill in directing group activity, has natural authority and gains respect of others. Capable of building an effective team. Involves all team members and gives advice and help when required.

However, these lists do not really explain what a leader actually does in order to produce the necessary response in team members: that is, what makes the difference between a leader and a non-leader.

As the idea of leadership is so important in modern day thinking on management, we dwell on this aspect somewhat as a special case, focusing on some of the problems associated with identifying manifest skills concerned with the business of managing other people. We will then offer some approaches to measuring leadership skills in managers.

The problem with the concept of leadership lies in its interpretation (refer to the discussion on skills language above). McCormick and Ilgen (1985) outline three different points of view of leadership which see it as:

1. *Positional*: related to the job and position that a person is in to exercise the power and authority which comes with the job. Little or . no credit to the individual in his or her own right.

2. *Personal*: where it is the personal attribute of the individual

which enables him or her to be a leader. This has given rise to research on abilities and other personal variables to distinguish between effective and ineffective leaders.

3. *Processional*: this focuses on the process of leadership and on what people have to do in order to influence others and achieve group goals. This process is obviously influenced by both the individual and the job he or she has (eg Katz and Kahn, 1978). The position of Katz and Kahn (1978) is that the degree of influence of a 'leader' exceeds that of simply applying standard operating procedures.

Related to these three basic concepts of leadership are three major theories of leadership outlined by McCormick and Ilgen (1985): trait theory (relating to the person); behaviour theory (relating to processional approaches); and situational-moderation theories (looking at contextual influences on leadership styles and effectiveness).

Trait theory was popular before the mid-1950s, but much research led to dead-ends! It was found difficult to correlate particular attributes and characteristics directly with leadership success. For example, although leaders tended to be strong on intelligence, social skills and task skills, the number of non-leaders possessing these traits was also large (eg Gibb, 1954).

Interest has been rekindled of late with such studies as Ghisselli (1971) and Campbell *et al (1970)*, showing that through a consideration of specific management positions, traits can be identified which relate to leadership success in the particular position. This is currently the basis of psychometric testing procedures for selection purposes.

Much interest has shifted towards behaviour theories and away from trait theories in an attempt to see how leaders are able to influence the group. The research has led to the identification of two major groupings of leadership behaviour, one of which is staff-centred, the other production-centred. Research undertaken initially at the University of Michigan has led to studies which show that one group of behaviours are better than the other (eg the Human Relations School which favours a staff-centred approach: Morse and Reimer, 1956) and have been developed into complete leadership 'systems', particularly the 'managerial grid' of Blake and Mouton (1985 for the third version). Variations of this have been developed over the years (eg Tannenbaum and Schmitt, 1973), but essentially studies have focused on what the present author would call 'styles' of leadership, which may or may not be appropriate in any particular situation.

The contingency model (Feidler, 1967) was developed, perhaps as a response to a need to incorporate the contextual arrangements of an organization in a relationship with individual styles of behaviour. From behavioural studies it became apparent that no specific behaviours were best for all situations: leadership is situational dependent!

Again, Fiedler's (1967) schema of leadership behaviour incorporates the task-oriented/person-oriented dichotomy of past work, but concludes that behaviour pertaining to these two styles is appropriate depending on the situation. The situation is defined in terms of favourableness to the leader where:

- the leader has greatest influence over the work group (leader-member relationship);
- a more structured task favours the leader situation (degree of task structure);
- The more reward/punishment the leader has command of the more influence he or she will have (formal power position).

The degree of likely success of leaders employing one of the two leadership styles can be analysed using these situational factors above. For example, where there is a high degree of formal power, a task-oriented or authoritarian style will be more successful. In situations which are neither favourable or unfavourable to the leader, a more democratic or people-oriented style will be more successful. Where the leader is presented with a situation which is unfavourable on all of the above three counts, then a more authoritarian style will be more successful.

It is perhaps with this in mind that we should appraise managerial skills and competencies. Particularly with leadership as an example, being so prominent a component of competencies lists. Consideration should be given to theories of managerial behaviour; particularly, the contingency model should be taken into consideration when looking at the skills language of an organization. This may answer some of the questions: 'what do we mean by effective leadership in an organization?'; 'what types of behaviour is appropriate in this particular organization?'.

We have raised these issues as a reminder of the dangers of going blindly down the competencies route. The issues are complex, but the problems are not insurmountable.

METHOD FOR MEASURING LEADERSHIP
BEHAVIOUR

It is possible to measure leadership behaviour in an interactive situation either by constructing a simulated situation in a classroom, laboratory or assessment centre, or by observing managers in action.

We have said that appropriate leadership behaviour may relate to one of the following groups of behaviour or leadership style:

- Task behaviours: characterized by the use of one-way communication, directing, explaining and information giving.
- Maintenance (relationship) behaviours: behaviour characterized by opening two-way communication encouraging and building trust.

The following schematic reflecting these two behaviour groups is adapted from Hersey and Blanchard (1977).

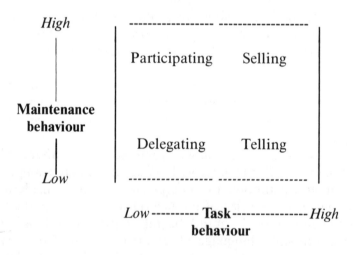

Figure 5.3 *Leadership behaviour*

The labels in the quadrant are typical activities or styles of the combination of maintenance and task behaviours.

Managers can be given a rating on the following instrument adapted from Johnson and Johnson (1975).

Rate the manager as follows against each of the behaviours described.
  With subordinates the manager exhibits this behaviour:
(1–Never   2–Seldom   3–Occasionally   4–Frequently   5–Always)

 1. Gives opinions and information   —
 2. Encourages participation.   —
 3. Seeks information and opinions.   —
 4. Compromizes and reconciles differences.   —
 5. Initiates action through proposing goals and tasks.   —
 6. Relieves tension by joking and relaxing others.   —
 7. Provides direction on the task at hand.   —
 8. Helps communication with and between others.   —
 9. Summarizes by pulling together ideas.   —
10. Understands group climate by asking others how they
    feel.   —
11. Co-ordinates and pulls together activities of the
    group.   —
12. Watches the group process and feeds back
    information for others.   —
13. Diagnoses problems and difficulties of the group.   —
14. Sets the standards of the group.   —
15. Energizes and stimulates a higher quality of work.   —
16. Listens actively and is receptive to ideas.   —
17. Tests the practicality of ideas in real situations.   —
18. Builds trust by encouraging openness.   —
19. Evaluates the difference between goals and
    accomplishments.   —
20. Solves problems of interpersonal conflict.   —

                                              Totals   *x*__   *y*__

Plot the score on the following grid on the x *and* y *axes.*

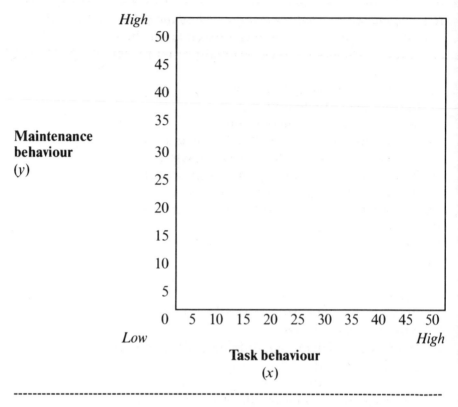

Figure 5.4 *Analysing leadership behaviour*

This grid may be used to both measure type of leadership behaviour against effectiveness of leadership in the organizational situation, and as a development tool. It is highly unlikely that any manager plotted in the bottom left hand corner of the grid is effective in any situation, and needs to develop the behaviours of both task and maintenance styles. Those exhibiting too high a task orientation may be ineffective in a situation demanding a high maintenance or relationship style. A general rating may be made on the general effectiveness of the manager as a leader in the situation in which he or she is being appraised, as follows.

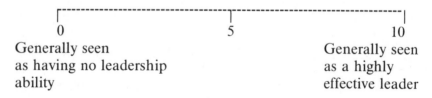

This can be compared with results on the grid to see which is the most effective group of behaviours in the current leadership situation.

WHAT DO MANAGERS PRODUCE?

Many writers deal with management characteristics and even management responsibilities, but few deal with manager's *products*. Hard but indirect products are *business results* such as:

- organizational efficiency;
- productivity;
- profit maximization;
- organizational growth;
- organizational stability (for example Miner, 1978).

Although, business results are ultimately the objective of business management, there is difficulty in linking directly (in a causal way) what a manager does and what the business produces. This is because managers achieve these types of products through the people they manage. Once they start to produce directly they cease being a manager and assume another role.

Reddin (1970) provides a useful classification on managerial effectiveness which has a bearing on this:

- *Apparent* effectiveness: extent to which a manager gives the appearance of being effective, for example by always being on time, having a tidy desk, answering queries promptly.
- *Leadership* effectiveness: extent to which the leader influences his or her followers to achieve group objectives.
- *Personal* effectiveness: extent to which a manager achieves his or her own objectives, for example gaining promotion.
- *Managerial* effectiveness: extent to which a manager achieves the output required of his or her position.

Although the last category does not give us much information, it does provide an important clue to a point that is going to be made quite forcibly throughout this text: that a manager's output or products *are* whatever they are supposed to be. In other words, management performance, and the results of this performance, are a matter of policy.

Nearly 20 years later Reddin (1989) helps to clarify what can and cannot be regarded as managers' output by reminding us of Henri Fayol's statement that authority must be commensurate with responsibility. In other words, a manager can only be held responsible for a particular outcome if he or she has the authority to influence it! A sales manager should not be held responsible for profits if he or she cannot decide sales margins or prices.

As an example Reddin (1989) uses a 'job effectiveness description' designed for a particular training manager, which illustrates the type of outputs he or she is focusing on, and how they relate to the authority given to the training manager:

Effectiveness areas (measurement areas)

- Identify training needs: percentage of personnel with training needs agreed.
- Meet training needs: percentage of personnel with training needs met.
- Behaviour change: behaviour changes leading to cost reductions per year as percentage of relevant budget per year. Behaviour changes relating to profit improvement per year as percentage of relevant annual budget per year; number of behaviour changes related to service improvement per year.

Authority areas – can make decisions on:

- frequency and method of conducting training needs analysis;
- type, number and sequence of courses;
- who attends courses;
- course design;
- whether to design course or buy in;
- teaching methods;
- whether to involve outside trainers;
- which training staff to be used;
- survey techniques to be used to measure behaviour change.

Reddin sees the things managers do as 'inputs' and the things they achieve as 'outputs'. Inputs for the training manager in Reddin's example, would be:

- knowledge of course design;
- knowledge of training packages available;
- motivation of trainers;
- training needs analysis.

As such, inputs are simply a means to an end, with outputs seen as the most important factor in a manager's performance. Therefore, competencies are largely unimportant provided that the manager delivers outputs at the end of the day. It is however necessary to look at this from a cultural perspective, as not all organizations are so overtly output – orientated nor wish to be changed to this orientation. As Jacobs (1989) points out, approaches in assessing management performance generally follow a continuum as follows.

Concern with process   'Conventional'
                                        competency-based
                                        approach

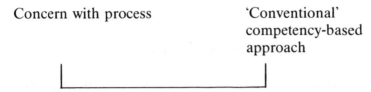

To the right will be more traditionally operating organizations such as the major banks, which are slower moving and where it is easier to assess an outcome which presents more of a fixed target. In the newer industries, such as the fast-moving high-tech companies, there is a stronger emphasis on the 'soft' process qualities of management (managing corporate culture, living with ambiguity') where it is difficult to define outcome across the organization and over time (Jacobs, 1989).

Staying with a cultural perspective, Kimura and Yoshimori (1989) point to the difficulty of constructing an individual job description (the corner stone of Reddin's, 1989, approach) in Japanese industry because of the undeveloped 'individual consciousness'. Work is collectively based, even for managers, and it is difficult to point directly to individual outcomes since areas of responsibility are not strictly defined.

This is the case in some Western industries and companies, where team working is emphasized and is indeed desirable for obtaining ultimate corporate results. Lessem (1989) distinguishes the soft and hard qualities of management as epitomized by 'co-operation' and 'competition' respectively (or *'yin'* and *'yang'*; or even right and left brain functioning). Although emphasis on these two aspects of organizational functioning may differ from culture to culture, they are present in varying degrees in all organizations. It is the hard aspects (rational, deliberate, results-oriented) which are easiest to measure, and the soft aspects (feeling, diffused, process-oriented) which are more difficult if not impossible to quantify.

However, results are important to any organization, and usually the bottom line for a commercial organization is the profit made or return on assets or capital employed. The issues here are: the extent to which individual managers can be called to account for results; what results they can be accountable for; and the desirability of focusing on results for purposes of measurement and development of management performance. This should not preclude focusing on soft processes in the organization, and it is argued later that a consideration of this aspect is essential in understanding what makes managers effective.

LEVELS OF RESULTS

We have argued elsewhere (Jackson, 1989) that there are three levels of results within an organization: at the skills level, at the operational level, and at the corporate level. Furthermore, it was argued that it is possible to develop a link (although not directly a causal link) between these three as follows.

Corporate results

↑

|

Operational results

↑

|

Individual skills

Any link demonstrated between these three levels must be tenuous (although not necessarily speculative) since the Fayol principle, pointed out by Reddin (1989) and, cited above, argues that authority must be commensurate with responsibility. Alliger and Janak (1989) also cast considerable doubt on the viability of a causal model of this sort when they examined the well-known Kirkpatrick model of training evaluation. We will examine these problems of methodology later in this chapter. Suffice to say here that these problems are considerable.

However, the model suggested in Jackson (1989) is a useful one for understanding the results for which a manager may be responsible. This is provided in the framework shown in Figure 5.5.

This model presupposes a rational approach to management where corporate objectives are propagated down the organization, and the line responds by aiming their activities at these corporate objectives. Perhaps this provides us with a good measure of manage-

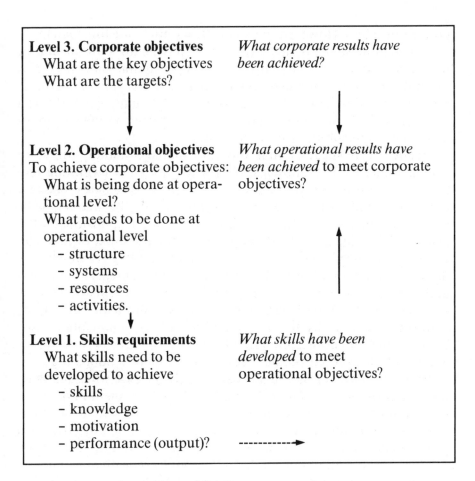

Level 3. Corporate objectives
  What are the key objectives
  What are the targets?

*What corporate results have
been achieved?*

Level 2. Operational objectives
To achieve corporate objectives:
  What is being done at opera-
  tional level?
  What needs to be done at
  operational level
    - structure
    - systems
    - resources
    - activities.

*What operational results have
been achieved* to meet corporate
objectives?

Level 1. Skills requirements
  What skills need to be
  developed to achieve
    - skills
    - knowledge
    - motivation
    - performance (output)?

*What skills have been
developed* to meet
operational objectives?

Figure 5.5 *Management results*

ment results: evidence of meeting predetermined objectives. This has
certainly been the basis of measurement in the management by
objectives (MBO) approach of the last couple of decades.

What the model does provide us with is an indication of management responsibility. To meet the operational objectives of the organization, the manager has got to ensure that the personnel for whom he
or she is responsible must: be trained in the required skills and
knowledge necessary to do the job; be motivated to do the job; be
providing a suitable output commensurate with operational objectives. The manager must also ensure, where he or she has the authority,
that activities undertaken, resources employed, systems used, and
structure of organization must all be directed towards meeting cor-

porate objectives. However, there may be a limit to the line manager's authority in these areas, and therefore it may be difficult for him or her to take total responsibility for the operational outcomes. For example, where the organizational structure of the line operation is not determined or cannot be changed by the line manager, if this is a factor in the outcomes of the line operation, then the manager cannot take total responsibility for the outcome.

Practice also suggests that the line manager cannot disclaim responsibility for operational results when not all determining factors are within his or her control. The example of a sales manager comes to mind: where there is a down-turn in the market, sales results may be poor but the sales manager is still responsible for the results of this department. Perhaps this is the dilemma of management: that managers are called to account for results over which they do not have total authority. To what extent can managers have total authority over other human beings and over world events which may influence their results? Perhaps this is the flaw in Fayol's principle!

In the final analysis, the ultimate result in any organization must be the achievement of corporate objectives. The link between operational results and corporate results is even more tenuous than the skills to operational link. This is particularly the case when management performance is seen as an individual's achievement rather than the achievement of the team as a whole. To what extent the sales manager has contributed to the meeting of corporate objectives is a problematic question. Obviously, without having sold the company's products, profit will not be made and corporate objectives will not be met. But the production manager has presumably also had a hand in this by achieving production targets; the personnel manager has overseen recruiting and training the workforce; the finance manager has allowed for sufficient cash flow; and the market research manager has judged the market well. But who is more worthy of praise? Who has contributed the most to meeting corporate objectives? It would seem logical to attribute this to the management team as a whole, with the chief executive claiming overall responsibility for meeting the company's objectives!

The objectives approach to determining management results is a useful one, but not the only model used in looking at organizational results as a whole. Cameron (1980) outlines four models of organization effectiveness as follows.

1. The *goal* model: how well an organization has met its goals (ineffective if the organization has ill-defined goals).

2. The *systems resource* model: the extent to which the organization gains needed resources from the environment (although organizational output is not a direct function of obtaining the best resources).
3. The *internal processes* model: an absence of undue internal strain; a healthy organization (it is possible, however, that organizations can succeed with internal conflicts and other internal problems).
4. The *strategic constituencies* model: the degree to which those who have a stake in the organization are satisfied (although different stakeholders, or 'strategic constituencies' who have a major influence in the organization, may have widely differing views on what constitutes organizational effectiveness).

So the question 'what are management results?' is not a straightforward one when focusing on the organizational level. There is no agreement on what constitutes a measure of an effective organization let alone an effective manager (making the assumption that the two – effective managers contribute to the effectiveness of the organization – are inextricably linked). Campbell's list of effectiveness criteria, Hodge and Anthony (1988:298) claim, is widely accepted as a comprehensive list of standards for establishing organizational effectiveness. This list includes the following:

- quality;
- growth;
- turnover;
- motivation;
- control;
- flexibility/adaptation;
- goal consensus;
- role and norm congruence;
- management skills;
- management of information and communication;
- profit;
- productivity;
- accidents;
- absenteeism;
- job satisfaction;
- morale;
- conflict/cohesion;
- planning/goal setting;
- stability;
- value of human resources;
- training and development emphasis.

However, Cameron (1980) warns that in selecting criteria for organizational effectiveness, consideration should also be given to the following:

- the domain of activity being focused on (eg internal or external).
- Whose perspective, or which stakeholder's position, is being considered.

- The level of analysis being used (eg the individual, operational or corporate levels).
- The time frame being considered (long or short).
- The type of data being used (soft or hard).
- The referent being used (eg normative, goal-oriented).

Neither organizational nor management results are hard and fast. What are considered results (or products) from the point of view of organizational effectiveness, may be subject to interpretation and different perspectives. However, rather than being a problem for measuring management performance, it is actually a factor which may aid measurement, as will be shown later, if we remember that measurement is an analogy of reality as discussed in Chapter One.

METHODS FOR MEASURING MANAGEMENT RESULTS

Criteria for measuring the products of managers in any organization must be negotiated in order to form a culturally recognized currency within the particular organization. One of the main benefits of this negotiation process should be all managers in the organization pulling in the same direction.

Ideally the formulation of criteria for results of managers should be propelled from strategy, through operational objectives and down to management capabilities and competencies (see p. 109). Unfortunately not all organizations are strategic in their planning and not all operations are oriented towards hard results.

The first step is to obtain information on managers' perceptions of criteria for their performance, from all or a large sample of managers within the organization unit (a unit being, for example, a department or a branch in a large company). The present author has used the following list, asking managers, after items on the list have been mixed up, to rank the ten criteria in order of importance in their organizational unit.

Criteria for management performance

Results

1. Getting the days work done.
2. Obtaining optimum productivity through staff.
3. Contributing to profits.

4. Contributing to organizational stability.
5. Contributing to organizational growth and development for the future.

Competencies

6. Having good knowledge of the job.
7. Solving problems and making decisions.
8. Motivating staff.
9. Developing staff.
10. Managing change.

This list can be used and analysed in a number of ways. For example, the author has used this in the management analysis questionnaire described in Section Three, with managers and their co-workers (immediate superior, peer and subordinates) to gain a perception of the agreement between colleagues. Where the manager has a different perspective to his or her immediate boss, this indicates problems and ideally they should get together to resolve the difficulties of assessment of work, which they may find exists.

A simple way to analyse this information is to take the rankings of each item, by each manager and co-worker, as in the example below.

Example

	A Manager	*B* Sup	*C* Peer	*D1* Sub1	*D2* Sub2	*E* Total (B–D2)	*F* Ranking
Items							
1	7	10	6	6	6	28	8
2	3	2	2	3	7	14	2
3	2	4	7	10	10	31	10
4	9	3	3	9	9	24	7
5	1	1	1	8	3	13	1
	--						--
	22						28
6	10	9	8	1	5	23	6
7	5	6	9	2	4	21	5
8	6	7	5	4	1	17	3
9	8	8	4	5	2	19	4
10	4	5	10	7	8	30	9
	--						--
	33						27

A comparison can be made between the manager's and the co-workers' perceptions by adding rankings for the items for co-workers B–D2. Then rank order the totals as in column F to give a comparison with the manager's rankings. Items 1–5 are results-oriented criteria, and a low total of rankings on these items shows a strong results-orientation. Clearly, in the above example the manager is more results-oriented than the co-workers. But if you add the immediate superior's results rankings you will note that he or she is slightly more results-oriented than the manager. The same applies to items 6–10 which are competency- or process-oriented criteria – showing that the manager is less process-oriented than the co-workers – apart from the immediate superior whose total is 35.

6 Culture in the Management Context

MANAGEMENT AND CULTURE: UNDERSTANDING THE RULES

A main theme running through this text is that management performance is open to interpretation by both the manager and his or her co-workers (superiors, subordinates and peers) within a particular organization with a particular culture (set of explicit and implicit rules by which people operate and inter-relate). If managers comply with these rules or views of the world, they will be performing competently. If the manager's view is at variance to this culture or set of rules, then either the manager will have to change or the organization will have to change.

That managers are able to interpret their roles presupposes two things: firstly, that predefined roles exist which are capable of being interpreted; and secondly, that a culture exists within the organization which requires roles to be interpreted or which allows for roles to be interpreted – a conformance or non-conformance to a corporate culture. We have already looked at the roles which managers occupy, but have said little about 'culture' and how this differs from management 'styles'.

There is not an easy distinction between these two terms as they often seem to overlap, but let us look first at culture.

The concept of culture is drawn from social anthropology with the classic definition of Tyler (1871): 'that complex whole which involves knowledge, belief, art, morals, law, custom and any other capabilities and habits acquired by man as a member of society'. A more modern definition, and one which is applied to organizations, is that from Williams, Dobson and Walters (1989): 'culture is the commonly held and relatively stable beliefs, attitudes and values that exist within the organization'. It is difficult to apply the concept of culture to an organization which is, after all, an artificial creation and one with a relatively short life-span. A useful delineation is therefore that of a strong or weak culture.

The degree to which the values and beliefs in an organization are defined, commonly accepted, and adherred to may differ widely between a new and an older organization, the type of business the organization is involved in, where the members of that organization are drawn from (eg in a multinational company this may be across many countries and national cultures), the top management styles and actions, and the perceptions and actions of the organizational members. Also, part of the value system of a corporation may be its looseness, the extent to which people can interpret and even break commonly accepted rules. The degree to which values and beliefs are shared denotes the strength or weakness of a culture.

Another useful concept about organizational culture is whether it is a healthy or unhealthy one. A strong culture may support top management or denigrate it; may be healthy and positive towards organizational goals, or may be cynical towards top management and therefore negate management objectives.

Hofstede (1989) describes culture as a mix between values and practice, whilst Williams, Dobson and Walters (1989) refer to beliefs operating at the unconscious level, attitudes and values at the reportable level, and behaviours operating at the observable level.

Hofstede (1989) has measured organizational cultures along the following dimensions:

- process-oriented versus results-oriented;
- job-oriented versus employee-oriented;
- professionally-oriented versus parochially-oriented (the extent to which members identify with their profession or with the organization);
- open versus closed systems (style of internal and external communication, eg the ease with which newcomers are admitted);
- tight versus loose internal control (formality and punctuality);
- pragmatic versus normative ways of dealing with the environment (flexible or rigid).

He has also noted different national cultural influences on organizational culture as follows:

- power distance (degree of inequality accepted);
- uncertainty avoidance (preference for structured or unstructured situations);
- individualism (acting as individualists or collectivists);
- masculinity (hard versus soft values).

Perhaps the most useful way of regarding culture is as a set of implicit and explicit rules, for example:

Explicit rules   *Rules about artifacts*

- Ties and dark suits to be worn.
- Managers only to use managers' toilets.
- Parking places allocated by seniority.

Rules about how people should behave

- Should deal with customers promptly.
- Should attend early morning meetings.

Implicit rules
- Should not be involved with a union.
- Should put in extra hours at home.
- Should be punctual in the morning no matter how late you were working the previous night.
- Work through informal network where possible.

Rules about the attitudes people have

- Be cynical about top management.
- Regard company as a good employer.

Rules about values people should have

- Can deviate from these rules only if not officially caught doing so.
- Stabbing other people in the back is frowned upon but justifiable if helps promotion.

There is no clear distinction between implicit and explicit rules (explicit rules are not necessarily legislated for in the organization). There is also no clear distinction between rules and behaviour (adherence to rules), and observing behaviour is one method of extracting the rules of an organization.

MANAGEMENT STYLES: INTERPRETING THE RULES

Generally speaking the behaviour (or actions according to the definition in Chapter One) of individuals is a combination of culturally guided behaviour and interpretations of role within that culture: in other words managers' styles. Styles are a combination of what the individual brings with him or her into the organization (eg national culture, family or peer influence), the way the organizational culture (rules) is recognized, interpreted and adhered to, and the way the individual actually enacts his or her role.

We can sub-divide management styles into overriding organizational management styles, learning styles and doing styles. Likert (1967) has referred to the management styles of organizations as management 'systems'. He identifies four management systems: exploitive-authoritative, benevolent-authoritative, consultative, and participative-group. He has published a comprehensive questionnaire (using his well-known Likert Scale) to elicit the required information from employees working under the respective management systems, using variables of motivation, communication, interaction, decision making, goal setting, control and performance.

Likert's concept of 'system' is of an all pervasive style within which the management of an organization is conducted. It is not a personal style but a prevailing approach to management which sets the scene. A manager working within a participative-group system would not perform well within an exploitative-authoritarian organizational system, unless able to adapt. Likert therefore describes situational styles rather than personal styles; the difference between the two will be examined below.

'Learning' and 'doing' management styles on the other hand, are a characteristic of the individual within a particular environment. Rather than being two distinct characteristics, they overlap considerably encompassing:

- the way managers learn;
- the way they work (eg plan, implement decisions);
- the way they relate to others;
- the way they relate to the future (eg manage change);
- how they regard performance (eg process versus results).

Classical management theory provides frameworks for viewing the way managers relate to work and to people through McGregor's (1960) *theory X* (economic orientation) versus *theory Y* (people orientation); and Blake and Mouton's (1985) 'concern for production' versus 'concern for people', as we have seen in Chapter 5.

Contigency theory (Fiedler, 1967) suggests that there is no good or bad style of management, merely appropriate styles to match the group-task situation. Reddin (1970) develops this theory, providing a model of the effective manager as having both 'flexibility' and 'resilience', and the ineffective manager as exhibiting 'drift' and 'rigidity'. It is the effective manager who can adapt to the situation by recognizing what is required without being swayed by circumstance, slipping and sliding from one approach to another. Reddin combines his concept of effective management (flexibility/resilience versus drift/rigidity) with a situational dimension of task orientation versus relationship orientation. In this way he develops a model (three-dimensional management) which looks at these orientations (situational dimensions) and how they relate to ineffective, neutral and effective management.

An effective manager in Reddin's terms would therefore be able to adapt from the exploitative-authoritarian to the participative-group situational styles (management systems) of Likert. However, it would seem unlikely that management selection processes were working very well if a manager found him or herself in the position to have to adjust so radically, unless the organization was deliberately pursuing a policy of cultural change!

The relationship between the organizational context – its underlying structure, rules and assumptions – and management styles is fundamental. We are pursuing here a concept of *performance as policy*. This also assumes that the actions of managers which produce management results (performance) are also fundamentally linked with both organizational context and managers' styles (interpretations and perceptions of managers). Let us now look at an example of this.

PERFORMANCE MEASURES: A CULTURAL VIEW

We have made the point that managerial effectiveness is essentially rule-bound, and based on what we have loosely called 'policy'. Policy does not necessarily follow a deliberate and overt policy decision, but reflects the system of beliefs and rules within an organization. This system of beliefs is manifested in prevailing corporate cultures and in individual managers styles, which mostly reflect the way they relate to their environment (structure and people) through time (a changing environment). They mainly relate to this environment through communication and they achieve results through other people. Once managers begin to achieve direct operational results, they are no longer acting as managers but as technical experts (falling back on their own profession). Of course many managers do carry on their particular specialisms whilst managing a section or department, but this strictly speaking is a duty over and above their duty to manage.

One exposition of the policy nature of management performance that is particularly useful in this time of globalization of business and internationalization of managers, is that of Lessem (1989). Lessem looks at the evolution of business and management over time and across the globe, outlining approaches to management in the West (US), the East (Japan), the North (Britain and Europe), and the South (Africa). He looks at: entrepreneurial management (early stage of a company's development and typified in the West); executive or rational management as a second, bureaucratic stage typified in the North, but also borrowing heavily from literature and business schools in the West; developmental management, often a third stage to break down bureaucracy and develop quality, and typified in the East; and finally, transformational or metaphysical management aimed at higher ideals, and being a final but continuing stage which is typified in a few international companies and possibly in the South.

The point being made here is that these different cultural approaches to management actually determine both the competencies which managers should have, and the nature of their results. Let us adapt from Lessem (1989), in Figure 6.1 below, what he calls 'attributes' of managers in the four 'domains' of management.

Function	Entrepreneurial	Executive	Developmental	Transformational
Physical	Hard work	High productivity	Intense interactivity	Energy flow
Social	Raw enthusiasm	Effective teamwork	Quality circles	Corporate culture
Mental	Native shrewdness	Management control	Manager self-development	Process and change
Emotional	Sheer will-power	Competitive strategy	Co-operative strategy	Business interfusion
Analytical	Improvization	Formal organization	Corporate architecture	Natural management
Intuitive	Market instinct	Analytical marketing	Planned evolution	Unlimited possibilities
Imagin-ative	Imagination	Systematized innovation	Corporate renewal	Spiritually based vision

Figure 6.1 *Lessem's attibutes of management*

These are close enough to what we have called management competencies to make the point.

To be an effective entrepreneurial manager you need certain 'primal' (Lessem, 1989) attributes of hard work, enthusiasm, shrewdness, will-power, an ability to improvize, an instinct for the market-place, and imagination. It is at a more mature stage in the development of an organization where a manager needs rationally to plan for optimum performance of the organization, and turn attention inwards towards greater operational efficiency. Team work, control, strategy, and analysis are all attributes which are required in this situation. It is only when organizations are unable to compete on a purely production basis – when attention turns to quality of product and quality of life – that managers need to be developmental in approach. Quality circles are a typical feature of this type of organization, and self-development is an attribute which can lead to corporate self-renewal.

Metaphysical management, a more difficult concept to grasp, needs higher ideals such as transformation at a global level (eg world peace, conservation of natural resources, *glasnost*) or a 'higher order' concept of corporate culture. Lessem (1989) uses, throughout his book, the example of the Bank of Credit and Commerce with its ideals of attaining world peace through permeating the international markets. The attributes are visionary and spiritually based.

What about the implications for management performance, and more specifically management products. For the entrepreneur starting and developing a business, profits are most important and directly reflect the entrepreneur's ability to achieve results. With rational management, and the exercizing of executive abilities, the efficiency of the operational unit is of primary importance. Making the most out of both physical and human resources, to use them for optimum processing or production, is all important where volume is paramount and the organization of resources is key.

For developmental management, it is the design and quality of the service or product which is central to management results. It is only by producing well-designed and quality products that a business can remain competitive in a highly discriminatory, selective and educated market place. We can also suggest that the product of a metaphysical manager is to achieve certain specified higher ideas. Schematically we can therefore represent management results, evolving over time, as follows.

Time

---$\Longrightarrow$

Profit   **Efficiency**   **Quality**   **Higher ideals**

Entrepreneural   Executive   Developmental   Transformational

We have therefore introduced a 'subjective' or interpretive element into the idea of management results, and have stated that performance is a matter of policy, and that both organizational culture and management styles are important to what is regarded as management results. This is important to the methodological approach we need to take in order to overcome some of the problems associated with gaining information on management performance. We will now consider those problems, along with an outline approach to take account of them.

METHODS FOR MEASURING CULTURE AND MANAGEMENT STYLES

We will see in Section Three that a measure of management performance is the compatability between the style of an individual manager and the culture of the organization. It is essential that managers understand the culture of their organization, and for internationally, or even nationally, mobile managers who may work in different contexts, to quickly understand the 'rules of the game'. Even if they are to work at slight variance to prevailing organizational norms, they must understand what those norms are and how much they can deviate from them without, ultimately, losing their job!

We will first look at a qualitative approach to 'auditing' the culture of an organization, and then describe a quantitative method of checking the compatability between organizational culture and individual management styles.

An organizational culture audit

Hodge and Anthony (1988) describe a way of looking at organizational culture through 'rites' and 'ceremonies' in the anthropological tradition, and describe particular manifestations of these indicators which the observer can look for, as shown below.

Manifestation	Description
Rite	An elaborate dramatic event, through social interaction, usually before an audience.
Ceremony	A system of several rites on one occasion.
Ritual	A standardized set of management techniques which do not usually give rise to particular results.
Myth	A dramatic narrative of imagined events used to explain origins or organizational transformations.
Saga	A historical story describing accomplishments of groups or individuals.
Legend	A handed-down narrative of a significant event, usually embellished.
Story	A combination of truth and fiction about a true event.
Folktale	A completely fictious narrative.
Symbol	Any object, act or event which conveys specific organizational meaning.
Language	A manner in which group members speak or write to convey meaning to each other.
Gesture	Movement of part of body to convey meaning.
Physical setting	The physical surrounds which convey meaning.
Artifact	Manufactured material objects used to facilitate cultural expression.

These categories demonstrate slight 'overkill' in the opinion of the present author since many of them can be combined. Consider those indicators of culture in your own organization and describe them under the following headings, bearing in mind their *meaning, interpretation* and *implications*.

• Those *ceremonies* that are conducted publicly.

- Those *stories and myths* about the origins and episodes in the history of the organization.
- The particular *language and mannerisms* used by organizational members which identify them as members of this organization.
- The *physical surrounds* in which people work, which are somewhat different from other organizations.
- Those *artifacts* or physical objects which denote identity or rank in your organization.

As an example of the latter, to denote rank in an organization in which the present author recently worked, the size of chair and the height of its back was used to denote transition from one rank to the next, where actual authority and pay were not necessarily an obvious indicator.

Another approach you may like to take follows on from the discussion of 'rules' (see p. 117). Note down the rules of your organization as follows.

Explicit rules

- What are the rules about artifacts?
- What are the rules about how people should behave?

Implicit rules

- Are there any implicit rules about the way people should behave? What are these?
- What are the rules about the attitudes people should have?
- What are the rules about the values people should have?

Deviation from rules

- How far can people deviate from these rules? What happens if they do?

A systematic approach to auditing a company culture is described by Schein (1985), as follows.

Step 1. *Entry and focus on surprises.* An outsider enters the group to observe and get a feel for the culture, and watches for surprises that are not expected.

Step 2. *Systematic observation and checking.* The outsider makes sure that the surprises really are surprises.

Step 3. *Locating a motivated insider.* An informant is used to give his or her assessment of the culture.

Step 4. *Revealing the surprises and hunches.* The outsider reveals his or her assessment to the insider to get their reactions.

Step 5. *Joint exploration to find explanations.* Accuracy of outsider's assumptions are checked by the insider and together these observations are used to explain behaviour.

Step 6. *Formalizing hypotheses.* Collaboration between insider and outsider to formulate statements about the culture, based on the data gathered. Hypotheses are used as models of the culture.

Step 7. *Systematic checking and consolidation.* The outsider can now formulate specific questions based on the information so far obtained, and can gather more systematic evidence based on questionnaires, interviews, and stories or critical incidents.

Step 8. *Pushing to the level of assumptions.* The hypotheses are validated and the model is tested by seeing how the cultural assumptions actually affect behaviour by a programme that seeks to drive or modify this behaviour.

Step 9. *Perpetual recalibration.* The model is fine-tuned – is tested on other insiders to see if it really does reveal cultural assumptions – but being mindful that for those who are unaware of cultural implications within the organization, this may come as a shock!

Step 10. *Formal written description.* The formal description is written down, checked, and kept current.

Matching management styles with organizational culture

It is possible to identify management styles as dimensions of particular orientations of management such as in the following.

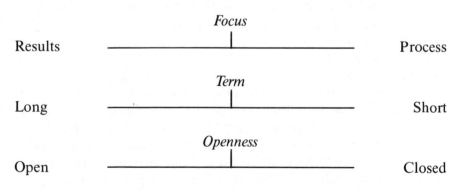

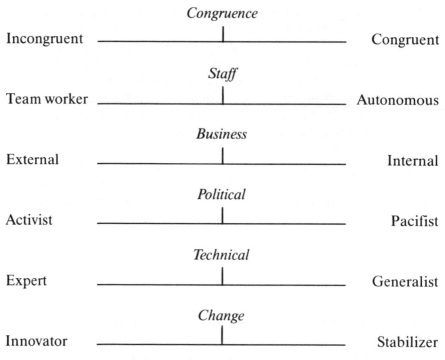

Figure 6.2 *Management styles*

No apparent distinction is made here between culture (rules) and individual styles (preferences and interpretations). The point being that it is possible to have, for example, a cultural focus on results or process, and a preference for either focus. The problem arises when you have a process-focused manager in a results-orientated organization: you will have a non-effective manager.

Some of the terms used above need explanation. Orientation towards the long term rather than the short term might be combined with a focus on results. More strategic thinking may focus on long-term results, whereas a sales-directed organization may focus on short-term results.

Openness is a function of participative management as well as honest individuals. There may be a time for 'playing your cards close to your chest' in an industrial relations situation for example, so there is no direct value judgement intended in describing a manager as 'closed'. Congruence denotes consistency and self-knowledge. A staff orientation denotes preferred methods of working which may differ depending on the nature of the work. Some managers may have to work autonomously whilst others will work as part of a team.

A business focus can indicate an outward facing orientation or an inward facing approach. This depends on the nature of the business and the level of management. Supervisory management may deal entirely with internal affairs, while top managers may be mostly involved with external relations.

Most large companies are rife with internal politics, but not all managers play the game. Often political activists gain promotion in such an organization, but in others, political pacifists (and probably outward facing managers) may get to the top. Some managers may spend must time on their area of technical specialization, whilst other managers may be developed as generalists and spend more time on managing proper.

There may be conflict in an organization between the need to stabilize and the need to change, with different managers reflecting each of these different orientations.

The following questionnaire can be given to individual managers for completion, or may be given to the management team for comparison and discussion of results. The emphasis is on the compatability of individuals' styles and the prevailing style or culture of the organizational unit.

SECTION ONE

Complete the following ticking one of each pair.

As a manager my planning decisions would be:

1	innovative	( )	( )	cautious	64
2	technical	( )	( )	general	65
3	political	( )	( )	a-political	66
4	outward looking	( )	( )	internal	67
5	staff-oriented	( )	( )	autonomous	68
6	consistent	( )	( )	rule-breaking	69
7	open	( )	( )	closed	70
8	long-term	( )	( )	short-term	71
9	results-focused	( )	( )	means-focused	72

As a manager I would tend to implement decisions:

73	tactfully	( )	( )	with vision	10
74	adminstratively	( )	( )	technically	11
75	non-politically	( )	( )	politically	12
76	for staff	( )	( )	for business	13
77	autonomously	( )	( )	through teams	14
78	by rule-breaking	( )	( )	consistently	15
79	close to chest	( )	( )	openly	16
80	immediately	( )	( )	over a period	17
81	as a means to an end	( )	( )	for results	18

As a manager I would tend to develop staff:

19	using new ideas	( )	( )	traditionally	82
20	as specialists	( )	( )	as generalists	83
21	to be political	( )	( )	a-politically	84
22	for business	( )	( )	for team working	85
23	as team-workers	( )	( )	to be autonomous	86
24	consistently	( )	( )	on *ad hoc* basis	87
25	openly	( )	( )	covertly	88
26	for the future	( )	( )	for immediate job	89
27	for results	( )	( )	to do their job	90

As a manager I would control work:

91	with rules	( )	( )	flexibly	28
92	administratively	( )	( )	by knowledge	29
93	non-politically	( )	( )	manipulatively	30
94	for team effort	( )	( )	for results	31
95	autonomously	( )	( )	through teams	32
96	by my own rules	( )	( )	by conforming	33
97	discretely	( )	( )	openly	34
98	flow	( )	( )	projections	35
99	process	( )	( )	outcomes	36

As a manager I would solve problems:

37	creatively	( )	( )	safely	100
38	technically	( )	( )	administratively	101
39	shrewdly	( )	( )	a-politically	102
40	commercially	( )	( )	internally	103
41	through teams	( )	( )	on my own	104
42	consistently	( )	( )	differently	105
43	openly	( )	( )	discretely	106
44	for the future	( )	( )	of immediate need	107
45	of results	( )	( )	of process	108

As a manager the results I would like to obtain would:

109	maintain status	( )	( )	innovate	46
110	be generalized	( )	( )	be specialized	47
111	be a-political	( )	( )	be political	48
112	be internal	( )	( )	add business	49
113	be own results	( )	( )	be team results	50
114	vary a lot	( )	( )	be predictable	51
115	be private	( )	( )	be public	52
116	be short-term	( )	( )	be long-term	53
117	be tangible	( )	( )	be intangible	54

As a manager I would reward:

55	new ideas	( )	( )	loyal service	118
56	technical skills	( )	( )	general skills	119
57	political acumen	( )	( )	loyalty	120
58	business results	( )	( )	team workers	121
59	team work	( )	( )	individualists	122
60	consistency	( )	( )	rule-bending	123
61	openness	( )	( )	discretion	124
62	long-sightedness	( )	( )	immediate results	125
63	good management	( )	( )	'hard' results	126

SECTION TWO

Complete the following, ticking one of each pair.

In this organization planning decisions are expected to be:

1	innovative	( )	( )	cautious	64
2	technical	( )	( )	general	65
3	political	( )	( )	a-political	66
4	outward looking	( )	( )	internal	67
5	staff-oriented	( )	( )	autonomous	68
6	consistent	( )	( )	rule-breaking	69
7	open	( )	( )	closed	70
8	long-term	( )	( )	short-term	71
9	results-focused	( )	( )	means-focused	72

In this organization the implementation of management decisions is expected to be undertaken:

73	tactfully	( )	( )	with vision	10
74	administratively	( )	( )	technically	11
75	non-politically	( )	( )	politically	12
76	for staff	( )	( )	for business	13
77	autonomously	( )	( )	through teams	14
78	by rule-breaking	( )	( )	consistently	15
79	close to chest	( )	( )	openly	16
80	immediately	( )	( )	over a period	17
81	as means to an end	( )	( )	for results	18

In this organization staff are generally developed:

19	using new ideas	( )	( )	traditionally	82
20	as specilaists	( )	( )	as generalists	83
21	to be political	( )	( )	a-politically	84
22	for business	( )	( )	for team working	85
23	as team-workers	( )	( )	to be autonomous	86
24	consistently	( )	( )	on *ad hoc* basis	87
25	openly	( )	( )	covertly	88
26	for the future	( )	( )	for immediate job	89
27	for results	( )	( )	to do their job	90

This organization expects that work be controlled:

91	with rules	( )	( )	flexibly	28
92	administratively	( )	( )	by knowledge	29
93	non-politically	( )	( )	manipulatively	30
94	for team effort	( )	( )	for results	31
95	autonomously	( )	( )	through teams	32
96	by my own results	( )	( )	by conforming	33
97	discretely	( )	( )	openly	34
98	by flow of work	( )	( )	by projections	35
99	by process	( )	( )	by outcomes	36

In this organization problems are generally solved:

37	creatively	( )	( )	safely	100
38	technically	( )	( )	administratively	101
39	shrewdly	( )	( )	a-politically	102
40	commercially	( )	( )	internally	103
41	through teams	( )	( )	on my own	104
42	consistently	( )	( )	differently	105
43	openly	( )	( )	discretely	106
44	for the future	( )	( )	by immediate need	107
45	by results	( )	( )	by process	108

In this organization the results obtained must:

109	maintain status	( )	( )	innovate	46
110	be generalized	( )	( )	are specialized	47
111	are a-political	( )	( )	are political	48
112	are internal	( )	( )	add business	49
113	are own results	( )	( )	are team results	50
114	vary a lot	( )	( )	are predictable	51
115	are private	( )	( )	are public	52
116	are short-term	( )	( )	are long-term	53
117	are tangible	( )	( )	are intangible	54

This organization rewards:

54	new ideas	( )	( )	loyal service	118
56	technical skills	( )	( )	general skills	119
57	political acumen	( )	( )	loyalty	120
58	business results	( )	( )	team workers	121
59	team work	( )	( )	individualists	122
60	consistency	( )	( )	rule-bending	123
61	openness	( )	( )	discretion	124
62	long-sightedness	( )	( )	immediate results	125
63	good management	( )	( )	'hard' results	126

Instructions for analysing the questionnaire

1. In the following analysis sheet you should cross through each number for which you have responded with a tick in the questionnaire. For example if you have put a tick in 1 for *innovation* in the questionnaire, cross through number 1 in the analysis sheet below, if you have ticked item 18 for *results* in the questionnaire, strike through number 18 in the analysis sheet.

2. When you have completed this for the whole of the question-

naire, count up each tick in the analysis sheet for each category. For example in *innov* (innovator) you may have crossed through numbers, 1, 19, 28 and 55. By simply adding the number of ticks this gives a total of 4, which you place at the bottom of the column for *innov*.

3.   When you have completed this process for the whole of the analysis sheet, for both sections 'You' and 'Organization', transfer the scores to the profile scales by placing a cross along the scales corresponding to your scores on the analysis sheet. For example, if your innovator score is 5 and your stabilizer score is 2 you place a cross five points to the left of the centre (0), and another cross two to the right of the centre point.

4.   When you have completed this process for the 'You' score, join up the crosses vertically to provide a profile of your own management style. Do the same for each 'Organization' score, joining the crosses vertically in a different colour to give a profile of the prevailing management styles and culture within your organization.

5.   Compare the two profiles to see how your styles correspond with those of your organization.

ANALYSIS

Add ticks only.

You

innov	tech	pol	ext	team	cong	open	long	res
1	2	3	4	5	6	7	8	9
10	11	12	13	14	15	16	17	18
19	20	21	22	23	24	25	26	27
28	29	30	31	32	33	34	35	36
37	38	39	40	41	42	43	44	45
46	47	48	49	50	51	52	53	54
55	56	57	58	59	60	61	62	63
--	--	--	--	--	--	--	--	--

stab	gen	pac	int	aut	incong	closed	short	process
64	65	66	67	68	69	70	71	72
73	74	75	76	77	78	79	80	81
82	83	84	85	86	87	88	89	90
91	92	93	94	95	96	97	98	99
100	101	102	103	104	105	106	107	108
109	110	111	112	113	114	115	116	117
118	119	120	121	122	123	124	125	126
---	---	---	---	---	---	---	---	---

Organization

innov	tech	pol	ext	team	cong	open	long	res
1	2	3	4	5	6	7	8	9
10	11	12	13	14	15	16	17	18
19	20	21	22	23	24	25	26	27
28	29	30	31	32	33	34	35	36
37	38	39	40	41	42	43	44	45
46	47	48	49	50	51	52	53	54
55	56	57	58	59	60	61	62	63
--	--	--	--	--	--	--	--	--

stab	gen	pac	int	aut	incong	closed	short	process
64	65	66	67	68	69	70	71	72
73	74	75	76	77	78	79	80	81
82	83	84	85	86	87	88	89	90
91	92	93	94	95	96	97	98	99
100	101	102	103	104	105	106	107	108
109	110	111	112	113	114	115	116	117
118	119	120	121	122	123	124	125	126
---	---	---	---	---	---	---	---	---

*Show the profile of **you** and **your organization** below.*

	7	0	7	
Change Innovator				Stabilizer
Technical Technical				Generalist
Political Activist				Pacifist
Business External				Internal
Staff Team worker				Autonomous
Congruence Incongruent				Congruent
Openness Open				Closed
Term Long				Short
Focus Results				Process

7 Management Motivation

McClelland (1987) points out that to understand an outcome of someone's behaviour, we have to first: determine that a person is responsible for the outcome; that it was his or her intention to achieve the outcome; and that he or she had the necessary skills or ability to achieve the outcome. He refers to an example of Heider (1958) of a man rowing a boat across a lake where the outcome (getting to the other side) may be determined partly by the wind and currents and partly by the individual rowing. If the man did nothing and was blown to the other side we could not draw any conclusion about his motivation nor his ability to get to the other side. If on a calm day he rowed vigorously to get to the other side, then we could say that he was intent on getting there, having both the motivation and the apparent ability to do so.

This can be understood within the context-content-conduct model introduced in Chapter Two, as follows.

Context
To what extent are environmental factors determining the outcome? (eg How strong are the currents in the lake?)

|

Content
What is the intent of the individual in pursuing an outcome? (eg Is the individual intent on rowing to the other side of the lake?)

|

Conduct
Does the individual have the necessary skills and ability to achieve the outcome? (eg Can the man row with sufficient strength and in the right direction?)

|

Outcome
Has the outcome been achieved? (Has he got to the other side of the lake?)

The overriding question here is *why* has a particular outcome been achieved, and involves the consideration of motivation or intent in the light of both environmental factors and factors of ability. In an organization this involves the interaction between organizational pressures and objectives, and the intentions, perceptions and objectives of the individuals who work within an organization. This involves the 'attribution' of causation by individuals within organizations, which we discussed in Chapter Two. In this chapter we look particularly at why individuals cause things to happen through a consideration of the factors involved in motivation. We follow this with a look at how motivation, and how the strength of management motivation, may be measured.

MANAGERS AS MOTIVATED AND AS MOTIVATORS

Motivation impacts both on managerial performance *per se* and employee performance (via the ability of managers to motivate), and therefore by implication on management performance. To perform well managers need to be both motivated and motivators. Of course it is not within the power and influence of most managers within an organization to influence the motivation of employees in all aspects. We can follow Myers and Myers (1982) in describing those factors which both motivate managers and those which the manager manages, and the relative control which managers have over these influences, in Figure 7.1 below.

Clearly, organizational management can affect those influences within the organizational structure and environment and can be aware and make allowances to affect those influences which arise entirely or partly outside the workplace, such as peer influence and personal goals. However, organizational management can do nothing to directly affect genetic influences other than through appropriate selection of employees, and possibly through training and communication to change aspirations and reassess personal goals.

The literature on employee motivation has an abundance of comparison between different theoretical models, particularly Maslow's (1954) and Herzberg *et al*'s (1959) models. These provide, as the above factor model does, an idea of what motivates people in different situations. For example, both Maslow and Herzberg *et al* had an idea of the need to satisfy more basic needs (physiological, safety and social factors in Maslow's scheme, and hygiene factors in Herzberg *et al*'s) before the higher order motivators could be addressed (Maslow's

Factors	Examples	Degree of Management Control
Organizational	Nature of jobs Physical/technical environ- ment Reward system Supervision Available information Organizational goals Organizational structure	High
Social	Reference groups Peer groups Work groups Role set	Moderate
Psychosocial	Needs Perceived abilities Aspirations Personal objectives Perceptual set	Moderate to low
Psychobiological	Genetic Nurture	Nil

Figure 7.1 *Management control and motivating influences*

esteem and self-actualization and Herzberg *et al*'s motivators).

Maccoby (1976) developed an idea of management motivation based on the different types of managers he identified, as follows:

Craftsmen: Traditional, motivated by work ethic and thrift. Likes process and likes to build. Help others do a good job. May go along with others' goals they do not wholly agree with. Seeks interesting work.

Jungle fighter: Motivated by the achievement of power. Peers are seen as potential enemies or accomplices, and subordinates are used to accomplish their ends. Jungle fighters build empires.

Company man: Functionaries deriving motivation from belonging to a powerful and protective organization. Are concerned for people and are committed to the organization.

Gamesman: Motivated by challenging ideas and taking risks where the game is to win. They are team players and identify with the aims of the company. Other people are not used through personal ambition but to accomplish organizational goals.

Maccoby's (1976) scheme is an interesting one since it points to individuals being different and being motivated by different factors. On most lists of management competencies there is a category of 'motivation': it is well recognized that managers need to be highly motivated in order to perform well. But this may mean different things for different people in different situations. Apart from being motivated by financial rewards, the craftsman is motivated by a problem to be solved, by the intrinsic nature of the work itself, by producing something of quality, working alone or in small groups with well-defined and structured projects. The positive aspect of the jungle fighter is the motivation to succeed in a crisis situation, largely through not building social interdependencies as they are not motivated by working with people for a common end. Company men are not motivated by risk taking. They are company-dependent and make good middle managers, since they are sensitive to, and motivated by, social interdependencies within the work group. They are good negotiators, motivated to mediate between conflicting interests. Gamesmen are motivated to win, and have the energy, and usually the youth, to achieve objectives through motivating the team. They like to be autonomous and are likely to go to the top in organizations.

Competency language within an organization needs to recognize these differences, clearly indicating what it is that is being measured: motivation for what? how is it exhibited? what is the end result?

Before we go on to consider how motivation may be measured, and how we can take account of individual and situational differences in the objects or outcomes of motivation, we must first look at what motivation is, and the factors which affect the motivations of individuals.

Kakabadse, Ludlow and Vinnicombe (1987) for example, tell us that an individual's motivation is a result of an interaction of needs, incentives and perceptions. The extent to which incentives at work meet the perceived needs of individuals is important. There is both an objective element and a subjective element here. The individual must earn enough money to satisfy basic needs, but what happens after this? How does the individual see his or her 'higher' needs, and to what extent are the incentives offered, and the incentives inherent within the job, actually satisfying the needs of the individual according to that individual's perceptions of the situation?

Both Maslow (1954) and Herzberg, Mausner and Snyderman (1959), as we have mentioned above, address the issue of individual needs, stating that the more basic needs have to be satisfied first before individuals can pursue and satisfy the higher needs of self-actualization, for example. However, the hierarchical arrangement which Maslow suggests cannot be rigidly applied. Kakabadse, Ludow and Vinnicombe (1987) offer an example of a university academic who, because of the changes in higher education, may not enjoy the job security of automatic tenure, and may be struggling to satisfy the lower order need of job security at the same time as addressing the higher order need of self-actualization through pursuing research and publication. This may be similar to a management position where job security is dependent on job performance and risk taking to achieve results. A bad decision may result in job loss: a good decision may result in praise, job success and self-satisfaction.

McClelland (1987) argues that needs are not necessarily universal as Maslow suggests, and through 40 years of research on human motivation identifies four major (measurable) motivational needs systems:

- Achievement motive: the need to achieve task goals.
- Power motive: the need to influence and control.
- Affiliative motives: the need to develop interpersonal relationships.
- Avoidance motives: an anxiety which motivates individuals to avoid certain experiences (fear of failure, and rejection, even fear of power and success, for example).

(Readers should note the rather careless use of the term 'need'. As a motivator, food may be a need: people need food otherwise they die. Social eating may not be a need but a desire. Sex as a motivator is not a need. You do not need sex, you simply desire it: that is, nothing bad happens to you physiologically if you do not have sex! Most of the time therefore we are talking about desires, which are factors in motivation, rather than needs.)

Murray (1938), preceding McClelland's work, measures the strengths of the first three of these needs systems by the means of self-report. The following items, which would not be given consecutively in a test, are provided below as illustrations.

Need for achievement:

- I set myself difficult goals which I attempt to reach.
- I only completely enjoy relaxation after successful completion of exacting pieces of work.
- I work hard until I am completely satisfied with the result I achieve.
- I enjoy working as much as I enjoy my leisure.

Need for affiliation:

- I am happiest when I am with a group of people who enjoy life.
- I become attached to my friends.
- I like to mix with a group of congenial people, talking about any subject which comes up.
- I go out of my way to be with my friends.

Need for power:

- I like to organize the activities of a group or team.
- I argue zealously against others for my point of view.
- I tend to influence others more than they influence me.
- I am able to dominate a social situation.

McClelland (1987) himself develops an approach to measuring the strengths of each motivational needs system, derived from the Thematic Apperception Test approach of Murray (1938). Using either pictures or descriptions of situations which may, for example, have a high achievement content (eg a picture of a person studying, possibly for examinations) or a neutral content which does not ostensibly indicate achievement, subjects are asked to write a story about the stimulus. The content of the story is then coded to give a score on achievement motivation (*n Ach*).

Stories may be coded as follows.

For each of the following characteristics found in the story give +1. Give −1 for non-appearance in the story as follows:

Characteristic	Example
Achievement imagery	'He is trying to do well in the exam'
Need	'He wants to get high marks'
Positive anticipatory goal state	'He will feel great if he does well'
Negative anticipatory goal state	'He will feel bad if he fails'
Positive goal state	'He is happy because he has done well'
Negative goal state	'He is unhappy because he failed'
Actions	'He has been revising every night this week'
Obstacles in the environment	'His friends think he is a swot for revising so much'
Help	'He has been given a lot of help from his teacher'

McClelland (1987) also provides coding schemes for affiliation and power arousal in stories, and provides an analysis of the same story on achievement, affiliation and power, where the stimulus is a picture of a man at a drawing board: 'George is an engineer who wants to win a competition' – +1 will be given for achievement. 'George is an engineer, working late and worried that his wife will be annoyed' – will receive +1 for affiliation; 'George, a famous engineer, wanting to win a competition to establish himself as the best engineer in the world' – will be given +1 for power.

There are doubts concerning the validity of such 'projective' techniques (perhaps the most famous being the Rorschach Inkblot Test which Aiken, 1988, ranks as fifth in usage of all psychological tests in the US, followed in sixth place by the Thematic Apperception Test) in psychological measurement, and many of these questions are raised by Kline (1986). A major criticism, apart from the difficulty in establishing validity for these tests, is that they try to measure too much – frequently the whole personality sphere. Functional tests are far more useful, focusing on specific aspects such as motivation, and particularly when they are related directly to a body of theory and a conceptual model. In fact this is the basis of all measures as defined in this text, as a specific 'analogy' of reality is being constructed, as argued in Section One.

We have therefore looked at some of the theory associated with different psychological needs of individuals. We started with an idea of motivation comprizing needs, incentives and expectations (after Kakabadse, Ludlow and Vinnicombe, 1987). We will now focus on incentives.

Incentives focus on the external factors of motivation, rather than on the internal needs or drives of individuals. This is the area over which the manager has more influence in motivating subordinates: making sure the incentives match the needs. To a large extent, recent work on this has focused on the satisfaction of needs within the framework of Maslow (1954) and Herzberg, Mausner and Snyderman (1959) (for example Alderfer, 1972). It is not the intention to dwell too much here on incentives at work, other than to mention those external factors which may be affected by managers, namely:

- *Job design*: the way a job is designed influences the amount of intrinsic motivation; that is, the satisfaction of doing a job well or the enjoyment derived from the job.
- *Participation in decision making*: closely connected to the way jobs are designed, the management style of the manager, and the structural communication arrangements within an organization, this may also influence the amount of intrinsic rewards derived from a job.
- *Promotion opportunities*: providing extrinsic rewards and satisfying a range of needs within Maslow's (1959) hierarchy, including increases in pay and self-fulfilment.
- *Working conditions*: satisfying more basic needs of comfort and well being. A prerequisite to higher order needs satisfaction.
- *Pay*: usually regarded as high on the list of extrinsic incentives of a job, and probably more complicated than merely satisfying Maslow's (1959) lower order needs. Money is also part of a symbolic system within Western society, representing a person's

'worth' within society. Money may therefore be bound up with higher order needs such as self-actualization.

Incentives are therefore bound up with needs. If individuals do not have a need to participate in decision making within an organization, this cannot very well be used as an incentive. Consideration should also be given to such motivational models as Maccoby's (1976) and McClelland's (1987) in deciding which incentives to offer which managers.

Theories based on expectations are more current. Expectancy, instrumentality or process theory addresses the question of how individuals make choices about which courses of action to take in order to satisfy certain needs. The answer expectancy theory gives is that individuals will choose a course of action (make a decision) by considering the rewards which they perceive, which satisfy their own motives, and according to their ability to successfully perform an act which will result in the reward. There are a number of models based on this theory, stemming mainly from the work of Vroom (1964), and developed by those such as Porter and Lawler (1968), and Campbell and Pritchard's (1976) valence, instrumentality, expectancy (VIE) model.

This theory assumes that individuals are rational decision makers, who will choose between alternatives on the basis of which course of action is more advantageous. The theory may present only one mode of managerial behaviour, which may or may not be appropriate as we will see in chapters 8 and 9.

The 'valence' is the anticipation of attractiveness of an outcome for the individual, or a person's desire to achieve a particular end. When the end is achieved it may not be as attractive as was thought. For example, on achieving promotion, which seemed an attractive goal to pursue, the reality was quite different for a manager who did not enjoy the new responsibility at all. Valence is quite a difficult concept to measure as there is a need to distinguish between, for example, the attractiveness of extra pay or a reduction in working hours.

Methods used to try to measure valence have been conducted through verbal reports and questionnaires which may be open to deception, and projective techniques where the attractiveness of outcomes have been deduced by the analysis of stories. Inference from choices made by individuals is also possible, and measuring decision time will provide information about the relative attraction of different courses of action (where decision time is quick then the relative valences can be assumed to differ significantly). However, all these measures simply provide estimates of valence and cannot measure in any precise way.

Instrumentality is the next element in the model. This is the likelihood that performance is followed by a desired outcome. It usually refers to the likelihood of a first-level outcome or the immediate effect of a person's action – for example improvement in job performance leading to a second-level outcome such as a promotion or something else of benefit to the individual – which is the object of the individual's action, or the reason for acting in a certain way.

Finally, expectancy is a subjective link which the individual makes between his or her effort in a specific action and its result. If he or she expends certain effort in a particular direction, will the desired result be obtained? Two main methods have been used for measuring expectancy. The first is to obtain verbal reports from individuals on probabilities. But the problem here is that individuals may be unaware of their motivations and the relative strength of each motivator, may find it difficult to compare these varying stengths of motives, and may wish to conceal their motives. Another way of measuring expectancy is to infer from choices that have actually been made.

Lawler and Porter (1968) provide the following model to combine the three elements discussed above.

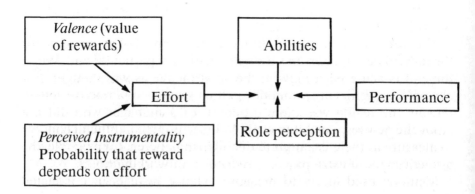

Figure 7.2 *Expectancy model of performance*

This is a slight adaptation of the basic theory and probably an improvement of it. Instrumentality is combined with expectancy to give 'perceived instrumentality'. Ability and role perception modifies the effort taken to perform adequately. Role perception is an attitude, and refers to the kind of activities the individual feels are necessary to carry out according to the way they see their role in relation to the desired outcomes.

We have therefore considered the three factors of needs, incentives and expectancies. Expectancy theory is difficult to convert to practical measurement application. Our main discussion on this aspect will focus primarily on motivators, and measuring strength of management motivation.

METHODS: AN APPROACH TO MEASURING MANAGEMENT MOTIVATION

The motivation level of individuals, both managers and subordinates, within an organization may be attributed to either the individuals or the structural and interpersonal arrangements with the organization. By implication therefore, performance may be a function of both the individual and of the organizational infrastructure.

The first task is to locate motivation within a scheme of causal attribution as described in Chapter 2, and as we illustrated at the beginning of this Chapter with the story of a man rowing a boat across a lake. Was he motivated to reach the other side, or was he simply blown to the other side? Can we attribute internal causes to his success, or external causes such as the speed of the current? In organizations it is often the case that the difference between external causes and those causes internal to the individual are not clear, and different individuals might have different perceptions of whether good performance is due to external or internal factors. We here adopt a method suggested by Stewart (1986), to analyse performance by reference to internal and external causes.

Using self-rating and superiors' ratings, a manager's current *poor* performance is assessed to determine the perceived source of the problem. That is, whether it is related to: internal or external causes, (an internal cause may be something the manager can gain control of); or is it something external to the manager where structural changes may be made in order to improve performance; or is it beyond organizational control? Examples of internal/external causes are:

Internal	External
• low confidence level;	• distressing news;
• poor attitude;	• insufficient opportunity;
• stress;	• unclear instructions;
• fear of failure;	• lack of support;
• procrastination;	• difficult environment;
• different set of goals;	• lack of authority;
• performance anxiety;	• inadequate resources;
• lack of knowledge;	• low strategic direction;
• Low needs arousal	• too much work;
• needs arousal inapproapriate to job.	• no recognition for job well done.

The following scales should be completed.

1. Does the manager perform other jobs poorly?

Internal   *External*

Always	Usually	Occasionally	Seldom	Never
X	X	X	X	X

2. Is the job performed poorly at other times?

Always   Never before

X	X	X	X	X

3. Do other managers perform this job poorly?

None   Everyone

X	X	X	X	X

If this hypothetical manager usually performs poorly at most jobs that he does then the cause is very likely to be internal. But if this particular job is the only one which has been a problem at the same level, then the cause is likely to be external. If the poor performance is really an exception, and usually the manager does a good job, then the cause of poor performance at this time is likely to be external. Conversely, if the manager always performs poorly in this job, then it is probably attributable to internal causes. If all managers perform this particular job poorly, then it is likely to be an external cause to the problem. If the current manager is the only one who performs poorly, then it is probably an internal cause.

We can put these altogether by joining the three plotted points on the scales as follows.

1.

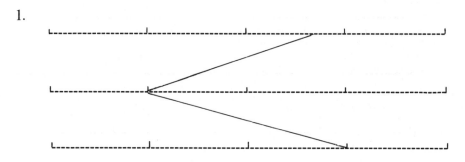

This pattern is a clear indication that it is an external problem of the job itself, and needs to be restructured.

2.

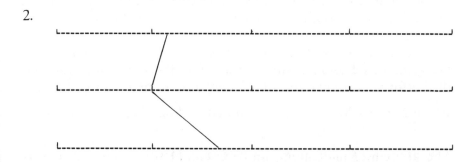

As the current job is being performed poorly, and others do not have a problem with it, the above pattern shows an internal cause of poor performance.

3.

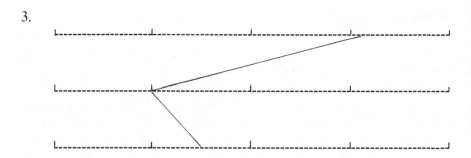

The above pattern shows that given that this is the only job giving the manager a problem, while others do not share this problem, it is likely to be an internal skills or knowledge problem.

4.

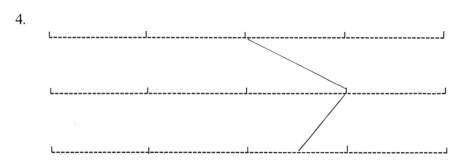

Some sort of external problem has hit the organization in this area, since the above pattern shows that this job has not previously been a problem to the current holder or other managers.

The method described will therefore give an indication of where the problems are coming from, and can be adapted to analyse good or poor performance.

Once an analysis of causality of good or poor performance has been conducted, and an estimate is made of the level of motivation in the performance equation, which may look something like this,

Performance = Motivation + Knowledge/skills + opportunity to perform

The strength of motivators can be tested. Despite their controversy, projective tests are useful where they are acceptable to the subjects completing them. Part of the task of constructing such tests is to make sure they have face validity, by being appropriate to the target group completing them.

We have already described McClelland's (1987) scheme as a useful theoretical and categorization model of motivational systems, and projective tests can be constructed to elicit responses in order to measure the relative strength of specific motivators.

Kline (1986) for example, gives some helpful suggestions of how to construct such tests. The present author has used these where they are more appropriate to the target group than questionnaires. However, questionnaires are a useful substitute, and readers should use Murray's (1938) example questionnaire items as a guide to designing a questionnaire (see p.66).

To construct a projective test, the purpose must clearly be defined, the relevant theory researched, and the necessary model constructed. McClelland (1987) of course provides a motivational model which provides us with categories of motives: achievement, affiliation and power.

The next step is to choose stimuli which are relevant and acceptable to the subjects. For example, with managers, photographs of managers in different situations could be used, from which managers can write a short story to describe what is going on. Alternatively, the beginning of a story or an account of a management situation can be given, or as recommended by McClelland (1987) the stem of a sentence such as 'A manager is sitting with an open file on the desk. . . ', and the subjects then have to complete the story.

The coding system suggested by McClelland (1987) may be used, or for achievement motivation, Heckhausen (1963) uses a simple coding system as follows:

- hope of success (HS);
- fear of failure (FF).

He also uses the difference between the two (HS−FF) or 'net hope', and the sum of the two (HS+FF), to give a score for achievement motivation (*n Ach*). Any phrase within the subject's story which indicates an idea of hoping for success – 'The manager is hoping to develop a strategy for developing business. . . ' for example – is scored positively, and any indication of fear of failure (although McClelland warns that there is no clear evidence that it is the opposite of the achievement motive) is scored negatively. The total score, after minuses have been subtracted from the pluses, is the *n Ach* score.

This is only a guide, and moreover a simplification of the method. It is recommended that McClelland's (1987) book is read thoroughly before attempting to put together such a test.

SECTION THREE

A DEVELOPMENTAL APPROACH TO MEASUREMENT

You cannot teach a man anything. You can only help him
discover it himself. (Galileo)

INTRODUCTION

In Section One we looked at the idea of a science of performance measurement, and its practical use in every-day management situations, and in Section Two we explored some of the work that has been undertaken in the various aspects of management performance. in Chapter Six we looked particularly at performance as 'policy', which has its roots in management style and organizational culture.

In this section we build a particular approach to management performance which looks at measurement as communication and as a means of development.

We first look at the importance of stylistic considerations to management performance, and the measurement of that performance, and then to developmental or processional factors and how they can be measured and influenced.

With the theme of making managers aware of styles and performance problems, and focusing on the key element of communication, we offer a novel approach to measurement.

The model to be developed is that of two broad dimensions of management which reflect the nature of management in practical situations – provides an understanding of why some forms of measurement work and some do not with particular styles of managing – and the implications of this for developing managers.

8 Conceptual and Intuitive Management

In Section One we looked at how measurement is an analogy of reality, a representation, and that measurement and its uses are acts of communication: communicating that reality as we see it, in a codified way by which we can gain agreement if our measurement effort is successful.

In Section Two we looked at the nature of management performance in some of its aspects, and how this reality of performance has been codified in order to measure it. We now summarize these main points and say how we can use this to develop an approach to measuring management performance.

WHAT MAKES MANAGERS EFFECTIVE?

Firstly we have said that there is nothing absolute about management effectiveness. There may be basic skills which managers can transfer from one organizational environment to the next, but it is the ability to understand and act according to the cultural rules of the game in any setting which enables managers to be effective. Therefore, the way in which managers perform is a cultural requirement: they are required to conform to certain rules (management styles) when they perform as managers; what are regarded as the results of their performance are a matter of policy within the organization, rather than being some universally accepted criteria across all organizations; the manager's ability to understand the rules of the organization is largely dependent on the communication processes within the organization as well as the individual manager's skills in communicating.

HOW CAN MANAGEMENT EFFECTIVENESS BE MEASURED?

It is possible to test:

- The implicit rules within an organizational setting.
- A manager's conformance to these rules.

- The amount of agreement as to what the rules are amongst co-workers; and by implication the effectiveness of communication (shared meaning) within the organizational setting.
- Those managers who are regarded as effective and those who are not.
- Management effectiveness criteria used by managers and their co-workers.

However, the implicit 'rules of the game' or managers' individual styles have a direct bearing on how effectiveness may be measured and how it may not. This is very important and means that as an act of communication, measurement is part of a social process. Not all forms of communication are effective in all situations, or produce the same results in all situations. Communication (remember we are saying measurement is a form of communication) involves persuasion if it is aimed at gaining results. Persuasion may have varying degrees of effectiveness; and so with measurement. We need to be aware of these processes and actually use them as a mechanism for gaining good results by measurement.

Active, pragmatic, entrepreneurial management (what Lessem, 1989, describes as 'primal' management – see Chapter 6) may not favour sitting down and filling in questionnaires. Different approaches to measurement will therefore have to be adopted depending on the particular style (learning styles, eg Honey and Mumford, 1983, are regarded here as being almost identical to 'doing' styles) of the managers concerned. This requires advanced qualitative information before a decision can be made about formal collection of data.

It is a problem that the types of methods associated with measurement techniques favour very much a 'rational' approach to management. This is a problem which the approach being constructed here attempts to overcome!

We have suggested that feedback of performance measures can help the development of management performance. This has substantial support in the literature as we discussed in Chapter 3. Again, the degree of effectiveness of this relates to the particular management style of the individual manager (as well as the culture or implicit rules of the organizational setting). Similarly, the way in which information is fed back, the nature of the information fed back, and the developmental use to which this is put, are all related to prevailing management style, and indeed to organizational cultures.

MANAGEMENT STYLES AND MEASUREMENT

We can paint a picture of a 'rational' manager as one who is happy to complete questionnaires, feels that psychological theory is useful to understanding management questions and one who can handle looking at conceptual models of how management should work. We can also paint a picture of managers who manage 'by the seat of their pants', who would not have time to look at conceptual models nor to fill in detailed questionnaires, and who would feel that psychological theories are irrelevant to day-to-day work. By using these two pictures of management it is possible to classify management styles and prevailing organizational cultures, firstly along the following continuum.

Conceptual ------------------------ *Intuitive*

Conceptual managers would find no difficulty in completing questionnaires, while intuitive managers may raise considerable objections. These two terms reflect both learning styles and doing styles, and have significance not just for collection of measurement data, but also for:

- the way managers learn;
- the way they work;
- the way they relate to others;
- the way they relate to the future;
- how they regard performance.

A further classification relevant to management styles and prevailing organizational cultures is the following dichotomy.

Congruent ------------------------*Incongruent*

In particular this has implications for the analysis of measurement data, but also provides a great deal of information about communication in an organization. Congruent individuals within congruent organizational cultures are more likely to yield consistent measures of performance since there will be a good knowledge of self, and good feedback on performance as well as consistency in feedback, allowing a better self-knowledge in self-rating and co-worker rating of performance. Policy on performance is likely to be clear and consistent. The opposite would be true with incongruent individuals in an incongruent cultural environment. There will be little consistency in performance measures, little agreement between co-raters, and no well-defined policy of performance.

Lack of consistency in measurement between co-raters over time does not present a real problem to those trying to measure management performance (although it would using a positivist model, see Chapter One) it simply provides a measurement in itself of the effectiveness of management communication: the most important aspect of management performance as we have already said.

Descriptions of these classifications of management styles and culture, and of methods of data collection and analysis associated with them, are as follows.

Classification	Description	Method

Conceptual	Rational management
	Process-oriented
	Happy with theories
	   or 'models'
		Structured interview
		Questionnaire
		Latitudinal studies
		   (across organiz-
		   izational units)
		Psychometric studies

Intuitive	Results-oriented No time for 'theorizing' Pragmatic	Shadowing Anthropological methods Longitudinal studies (over an extended
Incongruent	Poor communication Incongruent individuals Weak culture (identity)	period of time)
Congruent	Good communication Congruent individuals Strong culture (identity)	

Figure 8.1 *Management cultures and data-collection methods*

Since data collection methods have not been shown against the congruent-incongruent classifications it is the analysis of data from any method which it has implications for.

We combine these two bi-polar axes as follows, to explain the style of management and the type of data generated.

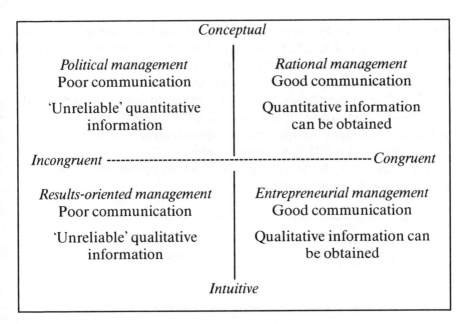

Figure 8.2 *Classification of management orientation*

For example, an organizational setting where most managers are happy to complete detailed questionnaires most of the time would appear somewhere in the top right-hand quadrant. This would indicate a high degree of communicativeness (consistent, good communication within the organization, giving a strong and coherent organizational culture or 'identity'), as well as a 'rational' style of management. Detailed quantitative information is obtainable. However, in the bottom right-hand quadrant, it would be consistently difficult to obtain good quantitative information, although qualitative information would be obtainable through anthropological research methods such as 'shadowing' or periods of observation and interviews with managers.

In the bottom left-hand quadrant there will be many of the characteristics of the bottom right-hand, but poor communication will prevail in the organizational setting, and poor intrapersonal communication within the individual (poor self-knowledge, incongruence). It is likely that only qualitative information will be obtained, and this will lack 'convergent' validity in conventional (psychometric) terms (see Chapter Three), but should be useful as a description of the nature of the organizational setting and its problems.

The management in the top left-hand quadrant, we can postulate, would perhaps like to be 'rational' managers, but in practice will be internally 'politically' motivated, probably inward looking, with poor communication. There may be suspicion evident among co-workers and felt towards senior management. The use of questionnaires may be seen as politically motivated (finding out information about subordinates), and responses are likely either to be guarded or will prompt an outpouring of the individual manager's problems with senior management. In any case, the quantitative information which can be obtained is likely to be unreliable.

Our model uses the following terms to sum up the general style of management in each quadrant.

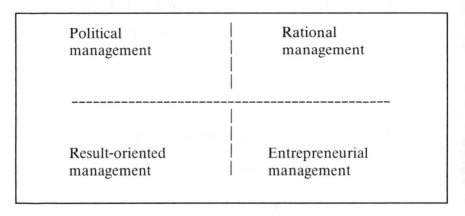

Figure 8.3 *Styles of management*

However, these should not be regarded as specific styles of management, but as classifications (or even prevailing cultures: remember that cultures comprize a set of rules, while style denotes an interpretation of such rules and a preference for certain perceptions and approaches) within which specific styles can be identified and summarized (see Chapter 6).

We have stated, then, that different methods of data collection should be used and different types of data will be collected, with different degrees of reliability depending on the particular broad culture and styles classification into which the organizational setting and individual managers fall.

The same considerations for the developmental aspect of measurement must be borne in mind. *Rational management* would benefit from feedback of questionnaire data, which is written and methodical, and might be happy with more sedentary forms of self-development. *Entrepreneurial management* will probably favour extremely short periods of useful, practical, hard-hitting presentations, the lessons from which they can apply in practice. Any feedback from analysis of their performance (which will be qualitative in nature, but methodical and credible) will be verbal and brief, as well as fairly instantaneous.

The two incongruent categories of *political management* and *results-oriented management* will probably have severe developmental problems, and will probably not be very effective organizational units. As a developmental goal, these two categories of management should be moving in the following direction,

Political management	----------------------➤	Rational management
Results-oriented management	----------------------➤	Entrepreneurial management

or from incongruence to congruence.

These different approaches to management may be further eludicated by a consideration of the following description and advice given to managers completing the management analysis questionnaire, to be discussed in Chapter 9.

Conceptual management styles

Political manager
This label means that you favour a *conceptual* approach to management, but you do not know yourself very well and you probably do not communicate very well. This identifies you as being *incongruent* and therefore in need of some development. This may not be your own personal development need, but a need of your part of the organization to develop better feedback and more cohesive communication.

As you favour a *conceptual* approach to management, many of the following descriptions will apply to you.

- You are quite interested in completing questionnaires such as this one, as you feel you might learn from it, but you may be a bit suspicious of it at the same time.
- You seem to learn from going on courses, and maybe also from reading appropriate books and articles, but you should not discount the benefits of learning in a pragmatic way from the job you do, and also from new experiences.

- You tend to plan carefully before you act and you like time to think about things before you commit yourself. You may need to 'think on your feet' in your job, but you may be uncomfortable doing this.
- You tend not to pre-judge people, but also (if you think about it and try to be honest) you are not always good at dealing with people, and sometimes misunderstand them or are mis-understood by others. You may think that studying people and reading about subjects such as psychology may help in under-standing people. You could be right, but you should also try to deal with people more on a face-to-face basis rather than standing back.
- Although the future, and the rapid changes in your company, do not fill you with foreboding, you may feel more comfortable with the stability of what you know. If this is the case you should try to strike a balance: learning from the present and planning for the future. You should be good at strategic planning.
- You are probably a 'process' person rather than directly results-driven. Of course, results are important to you, but you may regard your results as showing evidence that you are producing work or demonstrating knowledge of your job, rather than achieving clearly defined business results. You may not be very clear about what your results are and how you are judged as a manager. Do not lose sight of your objectives and management results.

It is unlikely that you are completely a *conceptual* manager as you will probably have some style characteristics of the *intuitive* approach to management. You may therefore like to read the descriptions for *results-oriented* and *entrepreneurial* managers, as well as for *rational* managers, which is what you are aiming to become.

As a manager who is leaning towards an *incongruent* orientation, you have certain developmental needs. Identify some of the following developmental areas which make sense to you, and which you can do something about.

DEVELOPMENTAL NEEDS
- You need to organize your learning rather than undertake it in a haphazard way. It would help if you share your learning with others at work, for example coaching others, acting as mentor to junior staff, or maybe organizing learning events at work. You

will benefit from this in both increased learning (for you and your protégés) and better communication.

- You should approach your work in a more systematic way: you certainly have the inclination to do this. Have you tried doing a time-management course? This may help.
- You should strive to become a better communicator, no matter how well you feel you communicate. This is particularly the case if others see you differently to the way you see yourself. Be more open in your dealings with people and do not be so suspicious of others' motives. However, this may be easier said than done: you may have grounds for being suspicious of others as they may well have political motives (in much the same way that you may have political motives). You must therefore ask the questions 'Is this a healthy organization in which to work? Can it be improved? How can I improve it?' Using this questionnaire may act as a catalyst in making people aware of the problems, but other organizational efforts may be necessary. Where you can, in your part of the organization, develop a good flow of information on performance by giving feedback and asking for feedback.
- Try to gain your own vision of the future. Take stock of your past and current achievements, and try to decide how best to use your strengths for the future requirements of your career and/or the business requirements of the organization. Learn to manage the changes which are happening in the organization.
- Communicate to subordinates a clear idea of what performance is required of them, and how performance may be judged.

Rational manager
Being a rational manager means that you favour a conceptual style and that you are fairly congruent. The latter means that you know yourself well and that you are consistent in the way you work. The idea that you have of yourself is also shared by other people you work with. This is because you are a good communicator and those around you communicate well. In some ways this management type is an ideal, and you should also read the description and development needs of the *political* manager in order to progress further along the scale for a rational manager.
The description of the rational manager is as follows.

- You learn best from structured learning experiences, such as developmental programmes,which are applicable to your job and future career. On the whole you are systematic in the way you approach your learning. You enjoy sharing learning experiences with others in your workplace, and you may organize learning experiences for subordinates and colleagues. However, you should not lose sight of what the business is trying to achieve, and the results you personally should achieve as a manager.

- You consistently plan before you act, in a purposeful and systematic way. You think a great deal about your job and you are probably a high performer in your current job. However, you cannot plan systematically about everything, and you should be prepared sometimes to manage 'by the seat of your pants'.

- You are good at not jumping to conclusions about people: you try to understand them and to be as open as you can with them. You are probably a good communicator, but you should strive to be a better one.

- Although you are good at managing change, you probably like stability, favour strategic planning, and find it difficult to react quickly on an *ad hoc* basis, or to improvize and take risks. You may have to do this from time to time, and therefore you should get used to it.

- You are fairly clear on what constitutes good performance, and you communicate this to your subordinates. However, this questionnaire may help to further clarify questions of your own performance, and to get agreement on it.

A DEVELOPMENT PROGRAMME FOR CONCEPTUAL STYLE MANAGERS

You will benefit most from formal and systematic management education and training which reflects the 'classical', rational, administrative approach of the business schools, and most management training existent in UK companies. This would include techniques and skills of management, and also the theory behind the practice, to give you a deeper understanding of managing people and resources.

Typical content of training programmes might include:

- motivation;
- team working;
- communication;
- leadership;
- delegation;
- decision making;
- problem solving;
- managing change.

Other business subjects which may be appropriate depending on your job and career

- business strategy;
- marketing;
- finance;
- operations management.

FURTHER CONSIDERATIONS

Styles and organizational cultures are not static, although they tend to reflect the type of business and function you are in. You need to consider if a *conceptual* approach to management is appropriate to your organization, or if it should be trying to develop a more *intuitive* approach, driven by entrepreneurial or intrapreneurial managers!

Intuitive management styles

Results-oriented manager
This means that you favour an intuitive approach to management, relying on your instincts rather than developing learning in a more formal way. You prefer a 'seat of the pants' approach to management, and on the whole, classroom styles of learning bore you.

The implications of your being a results-oriented manager rather than an entrepreneurial manager means that you have certain developmental needs which will be addressed below. This is because you have an incongruent orientation, and this will be explained in the description below.

Your style of management can be described as follows.

- The way you learn is by experiencing the job, not by sitting in a classroom, which you may see as a distraction from the real learning which you can only get by 'doing'. However, you probably learn in a very haphazard way, and you probably need to improve this by deliberately seeking new challenges and learning from these. It would also be a good idea to try to pass on some of your learning to others. Try to work more in a team: involve others in new challenges with you.

- You tend to take things as they come, which may enable you to react quickly to change. However, as you have an incongruent orientation, you may not like change very much as you do not feel very much in charge. You may even see change as a threat. This may be largely due to the lack of good communication within your organizational unit. You should do your best to address this situation, to see where this can be improved.
- In your dealings with people you may be quick to judge. This may not be a bad thing if you are usually right about people. However, if your own communication abilities need to be improved, it is possible that you are sometimes wrong about people. You need therefore to give yourself time before pre-judging others. Be more open in your dealings with others, and do not be overly suspicious of them, unless you feel you have good cause!
- You set yourself goals, but these may be very short-term as you have little idea of what the future holds. Try to gain a vision of the future, and work towards this, taking it a step at a time by reaching your short-term targets, and then working towards longer-term goals.
- You are results-oriented and like your subordinates to show results. Are you clearly communicating to them what you expect? Are you clear in your own mind what you expect from them?

DEVELOPMENT NEEDS

As a *results-oriented* manager you should be striving to become more *congruent* and more of an *entrepreneur* in style if this fits in with the organization. Clearly if you are strongly *intuitive* and your organization is strongly *conceptual* then you may be in the wrong job. Also, consider that you may not be totally *intuitive* and that you have some characteristics of a *conceptual* approach. So also look at the descriptions and development needs of the political manager as well.

You are likely, as a *results-oriented* manager, to have some of the following development needs.

- You learn in a haphazard way, and should establish a deliberate policy of looking for new challenges which you can learn from. Is yours the type of organization in which this can happen? Can you develop a 'project' which achieves results for the organization, as well as helps you learn from new experiences? Where you can bring in others to work with you learn from each other, or take subordinates 'under your wing' as their mentor so that you can share your learning.

- Try managing your time and resources a bit better, being more organized in your approach to work. Goal-setting may help, or even a time management course. Do not forget that courses may be useful to you if you can find one's with the right 'dynamic' approach which you prefer.

- Practice communicating with others. Walk around and talk to others to find out what their problems are (without being nosey). However, if your subordinates are not used to your doing this, you may find some resistance so take it slowly at first. Be more open with people generally. If you are in a competitive situation with others, to what extent is this getting in the way of the effectiveness of the organization? Is this something which can be discussed with other managers and your superior to see if more co-operation can be generated?

- Is there little long-term understanding of the future in your organization? If so, this may be a result of the nature of your industry and rapid changes which are taking place. But is this disrupting the effectiveness of people and the organization? Are managers openly discussing what they know, or is there a problem with communication? How much are you telling your subordinates? Have you got your own vision of the future which you are trying to work towards? These are some of the issues which you should be addressing.

- You should agree with your superiors and subordinates what constitutes good performance, since there may be disagreement. Once there is agreement, then everybody will be pulling in one direction.

Entrepreneurial manager

Being an *entrepreneurial* manager means that you are a fairly *congruent* manager with an *intuitive* style. This is what all *results-oriented* managers should be striving towards. Whether you are in an entrepreneurial position, or whether you are in a small or large organization, you can still be an *entrepreneurial* manager, although the popular term today is 'intrapreneur' for those exhibiting this style of management in large, mature organizations. Generally speaking the characteristics are as follows.

- You are very effective at learning directly from experience, you enjoy new experience and a challenge, and you actively seek out opportunities which will challenge your ingenuity. You probably would have little time for filling out such question-naires as this one: you may see the point for others, but not for you.

- Because you can 'think on your feet' you can react very swiftly to new circumstances and rapid change. You can grasp oppor-tunities, having both the ingenuity and motivation to do this: you can make things happen.
- You work effectively through other people, sizing them up very quickly, motivating them and achieving results through them. You have little time for formal theories about how to deal with people, as you work upon intuition and this always seems to work.
- You can see past the short term, and you have a positive vision of the future. You do not mind taking calculated risks to work towards this vision, as well as demonstrating shorter-term results. Change does not bother you as you see this as a chal-lenge, and you can motivate others to see change as such.
- You probably believe that a manager's instincts are more important that education and training, and care more for results rather than what is needed to obtain those results. But you should not forget that sometimes it is appropriate to have the time to reflect on what you are trying to achieve, and to try to further develop those skills you require, either on or off the job.

A DEVELOPMENT PROGRAMME FOR INTUITIVE STYLE MANAGERS

You will benefit most from challenging new experiences, largely on the job, but also away from the continual interruptions of the tele-phone and your trouble-shooting role as manager. Conventional business school courses will probably not suit you. The follow may interest you and provide benefit to you and your organization.

- Case studies of successful entrepreneurs in the 'in search of excellence' mould – you may enjoy reading these already.
- Developing entrepreneur/intrapreneur programmes of the 'hands-on' variety, using management games and simulations which challenge.
- Outdoor learning programmes which offer new and different experiences to develop leadership, decision making and risk taking.

- Project management: on-the-job experience addressing an organizational problem or development opportunity, which is used both as a learning experience and as a real task and opportunity for the organization.
- Giving lectures: short input (eg up to one hour) to colleagues, subordinates or outsiders, to improve understanding and aid learning for the lecture giver, and to share information and ideas with others.
- Networking: developing contacts with other managers in the organization for mutual benefits. Set a target for contacting new managers each week.
- Keep fit, reduce stress, manage conflicts, and develop an assertive approach to dealing with others.

FURTHER CONSIDERATIONS

You should look very closely at the organizational unit you work in to see if your intuitive approach is compatible with the culture and prevailing styles of organization. Is it possible or desirable to change it? If not, is it possible to make a career move!

It is clear from the preceding descriptions and advice that managers are different, and that we can use different analogies to try to encapsulate those differences. Lessem's (1989) analogy (discussed in Chapter 6) is one: the one used in this text is another. It is probably pointless to take the anarchic view that all managers are *completely* different: that therefore there is no such thing as generic management competencies, and that you must start completely afresh in each organization, generating new competencies, and taking account of individual differences. If we can allow for differences which may occur, such as in Lessem's analogy or in the current model, then this will make our job easier in developing competency lists in organizations, providing that the model used makes sense to the practising managers in that organization.

Let us now look at a list of competencies which has been tentatively drawn up in response to initial research, and to the demands of consulting in different types of organizations, and with different types of managers.

The list should be read down the middle, with the descriptions either side for intuitive approaches (left-hand side) and conceptual approaches (right-hand side), and with the generic competencies down the centre. The list begins with a prerequisite for managers, particularly at the junior end: 'Is able to: intelligently use a superior technical knowledge', and the description which follows is common for intuitive and conceptual managers. It then finishes with a 'bridge' between the two types of management, which managers at the senior end should strive towards: ' Is able to: be adaptable'. Here is the list.

Competencies

Intuitive   Conceptual

Is able to:

Intelligently use a superior technical knowledge

Has a superior knowledge of the appropriate technical area of current job

Motivate

self

Is motivated to achieve results involving some risk taking

Is motivated to achieve well-defined goals by following procedures

Has high energy level

Has tenacity

others

Can motivate others by being persuasive in an unstructured situation

Can motivate others in a structured environment

Make appropriate decisions

Through knowledge and awareness

Has an acute business sense

Is sensitive to the changing needs and problems of the organization

<table>
<tr><td align="center">Intuitive</td><td align="center">Conceptual</td></tr>
</table>

By analysis

Makes quick but sound decisions based on information immediately available

Able to think on feet

Makes sound decisions based on careful analysis and deliberation of information collected

By projection

Is able to pursue goals flexibly

Is able to plan systematically

Creatively

Is innovative, proactive and resourceful in approach

Is able to exercize critical judgement, showing initiative in response to situations as they occur

By problem solving

Solves problems rapidly in high stress situations

Solves problems effectively by careful consideration of facts

Communicate effectively

Interpersonally

Has strong impact on first meeting

Is able to influence others in a professional relationship

In a team

Is able to lead a team to achieve high results through setting high objectives

Develops sound team relations to achieve high results

Intuitive   Conceptual

Orally

Is a high impact speaker   Is able to present orally a
                                                  sound and persuasive case

Take on learning and manage change

By self development

Learns rapidly by undertaking   Learns rapidly in a structured
the job and solving problems as   way both off and on the job
they occur

By working effectively in a changing environment

Identifies opportunities to   Reacts positively to a changing
change methods of working   environment, and develops
where this will lead to results   others for new situation

Achieve results

With regard to process

Acts independently according   Considers prevailing social and
to own convictions rather than   ethical norms and standards
being influenced negatively by   of the job in striving towards
others in striving for results   results

Maintains integrity

With regard to results

Identifies opportunities which   Sets goals in line with organ-
will result in highest return   izational expectations

Contributes to organizational   Contributes to organizational
change and development   stability and growth

Intuitive	Conceptual

Be adaptable

By maintaining effectiveness in very different
organizational situations, roles and tasks

By rising above the immediate issues
and seeing the broader implications

To measure management performance we must, therefore, take
account of, and integrate the idea of, 'performance as policy'. This
looks specifically at the diversity across organizational cultures and
management styles. However, what this dimension does not take
account of is the dynamic of management: the communication
between individuals in a social situation over time. We are now going
to look at this dimension in more detail in the next chapter, by focusing
on communication as the central pivot in cultural diversity and
change over time.

9 Communication Management: Measuring and Developing Managers

A PROCESS APPROACH

Starting from a stylistic approach in Chapter Eight, and focusing on 'performance as policy', we now look at constructing a methodology which particularly addresses the process of management, with a major focus on the communicational nature of management which we have so far discussed. We have characterized these processes in Chapter Eight as: change over time and cultural diversification. For the practising manager these reflect current business trends of internationalizion of business, associated changes in doing business, and new technology and demographic shifts.

The implications of taking a process approach are as follows:
1. Data collection methods may be different for managers and companies in different stages in their development, and with different cultural make-ups.
2. Results from analysing data may be different, with different degrees of reliability and validity.
3. Measurement is seen as a communication tool which is part of a development process.
4. Both process and product (end result) measures should be taken of management performance.
5. As performance is regarded as policy, and measurement as communication, agreement should be obtained on the policy, and measurement (as communication) can help in this.
6. Competencies do not 'belong' to the individual in a communication process, but the group process has an impact on what the individual manager actually does.

Point 3., in particular, needs further elaboration. As in a process of rapid change, where the goal posts are continually moving, measuring is like 'trying to shoot a moving target'. Managers may know what is expected of them today (or more accurately yesterday), but may be unsure of what is expected of them to meet their organization's changing strategy, or to meet the needs of their every-day jobs. This may not necessarily be a result of top management's inability to formulate company strategy, but the result of a growing complexity and ambiguity in the market-place. Smiley (1989), for example, points out the decreasing usefulness of 'strategic management' as a means of managing a corporation in a period of uncertainty and rapid change. He suggests that strategy is useful for those companies which wish to be firmly managed, are hierarchical, are stable in their performance, and require long lead times for change. Strategy is reflected at the behavioural level in the organization, in sets of explicit procedures designed to guide human behaviour, rewarding conformity and reducing risk. Strategic management is based mainly on retrospective perspectives and works well when the future is a copy of the past (Hurst, 1986). There is perhaps a need to focus more on the processes of change rather than on end results, for example, where the company should be in five years time. There is a need to manage uncertainty. Particularly, there is a need to create a 'learning organization' (Argyris and Schon, 1978; Garratt, 1987).

Measurement is seen here as a tool of communication which can effect attitudinal shifts in thinking by providing feedback in a development process, which can then help managers clarify what is required of them in the future and reduce uncertainty.

This chapter outlines an approach which takes account of the five points above, and builds on the model described in Chapter 8. Rather than simply reviewing a number of methodological approaches, it points to a particular approach to measurement, based on the underlying concepts introduced so far in this text. Of particular importance to the way we measure management performance is the view of measurement as communication. This we now explore.

MEASUREMENT AS COMMUNICATION

Measurement, as we have said, is a form of communication. This particular form of communication represents a high degree of coding. The degree of coding involved in measurement may or may not be compatible with any particular organizational culture and style of management.

This assertion must be explained in some detail using the pioneering work of Shannon and Weaver (1949) in the field of communication theory, and its elaboration in the field of corporate culture in the work of Boisot (1987). Shannon and Weaver (1947) discuss three main problems of communication: the *technical* problem, the *semantic* problem, and the *effectiveness* problem.

The technical problem is that of the message at its destination not being the same as at its source. Solving this involves the capacity to transmit a message without encountering too much 'noise' or outside interference: by introducing redundancy or repetition into the message and reducing 'entropy' or that which is new in the message. At a corporate level, the questions might be: is the strategic direction transmitted by the managing director reaching the lower levels of the hierarchy?; Are appropriate communication structures in place to allow this to happen?; are there clear channels of communication?; is more than one channel being used to introduce redundancy and increase the certainty of the message getting to its destination? These are some of the questions which may be asked in connection with the technical problem.

The semantic problem is concerned with whether the message received is understood. Using a simple example, if the message received by a French manager is in English and the French manager does not understand English, he or she will not understand the message. At a more complex level, values may differ and therefore the message may be misunderstood. For example, certain commercial practices may differ from country to country and this may lead to misunderstandings.

The effectiveness problem is that of the message, once received and understood, leading to the desired behaviour. This is the problem with much advertizing. The message may be received and understood, but may not necessarily lead to the desired consumer response. To address the problem of effectiveness, it is necessary for the sender of the message to find out as much as possible about the receiver of the message; particularly those factors which motivate the receiver.

To understand better the interaction of these problems of communication, Boisot (1987) constructs a 'cultural space' from two important dimensions of communication:

Codified---------------------------Uncodified
Diffused--------------------------Undiffused

Firstly, information differs in its degree of codification. Numbers, for example, are highly codified, whereas personal information about feelings, artistic impression or values are uncodified. We can think of codified information as that which can be easily set out on paper for transmission, and uncodified information as being information which cannot easily be set out on paper. On a continuum from codified to uncodified we might have: numbers, writing, words and gestures, as media of information. Cultural values within an organization are not very easy to codify, whereas financial information is easily codifiable, and easy to transmit from country to country using modern technology.

Secondly, information may be diffused and shared among a certain population, or it may be either deliberately or unintentionally not shared and undiffused. This may, for example, mean that some information is kept secret within an organization. Information about redundancies in a company may be held only by the executive and not shared with the people it may affect. Values within an organization may be unintentionally not shared, and therefore will not act to unite the company.

Boisot (1987) represents these dimensions of communication in a two-dimensional cultural space as follows.

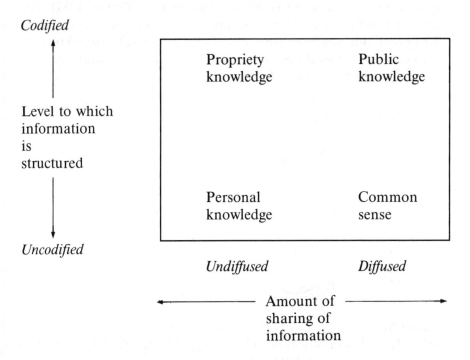

Figure 9.1 *Boisot's communication model*

Information which is uncodified and undiffused might take the form of personal knowledge, or biographical information about self which is not easily shared. Information which is highly codified and not shared may be specialist information for which a company has paid a lot of money to acquire and is too valuable to diffuse. However, once this information is suitable for wider publication – for example, a specialist who wishes to share his knowledge through the writing of a book – it becomes public knowledge which is easily accessible to anyone providing they know the code (for example you need to know something of mathematical codes before you can understand an advanced book on mathematics).

Common sense is an example of what is known generally but is uncodified. It is therefore difficult to pin down or quantify. Within an organization, the assumptions and values are implicit but are held in common.

Let us now look at the communication problems discussed by Shannon and Weaver (1947) within the context of the analogic cultural space created by Boisot's (1987) two dimensions. Boisot (1987) illustrates the technical problem by relating the degree of codification to the potential to share information within a cultural space. Thus, the plotted line *A* below shows us that the higher the level of codification, the more information can be shared .

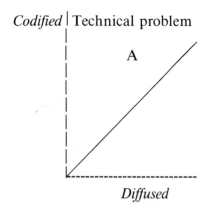

Codified | Technical problem

A

Diffused

Line *A* therefore equals the potential audience which can be reached for each level of codification. This seems to bode well for the position taken on measurement here. That is, the more you can codify performance (quantitatively measure it), the more potential there is for people within an organization to share perceptions of what performance is. This will therefore aid communication within an organization, and help development. However, things are not quite as simple as this, as we can illustrate by recourse to Shannon and Weaver's (1947) semantic problem.

Boisot (1987) represents this problem in the cultural space as the plotted line *B* below.

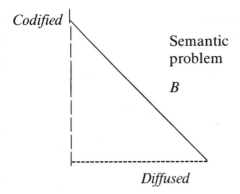

This represents the population competent to understand the message, and shows that the competent audience is inversely related to the level of coding. This is because codes have to be learnt. The easier the code the easier it is to learn.

This is probably why utility analysis (for example Cascio and Ramos, 1986) has not enjoyed commercial popularity as a method of assessing the value of performance, despite its academic attractions: it is simply too statistically complicated to understand (see Jackson 1989).

Also, line *B* shows that the more uncodified the message the higher the potential audience. This relates back to the case of 'common-sense'. There are more people in a cultural population holding 'common-sense' views about life than there are people understanding higher mathematics. However, unless there is a degree of coding, it is impossible to determine whether the common-sense views of one person in a population are the same as another. Mathematical information is easy to transmit, even between cultures, with an assurance that the transmitter and receiver share an accuracy of understanding once they have both invested in learning the code. A good illustration of this is the ease with which financial information can be sent round the globe by computer link, from one stock exchange to another, and be understood by people of different cultures and speaking different languages.

Finally, Boisot (1987) illustrates Shannon and Weaver's (1947) effectiveness problem in the cultural space by the plotted line *C* below.

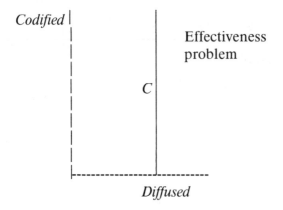

Line *C* represents the interested audience: the number in the population who will take up the message and act on it. If we assume the level of diffusion represents the number of people in the population who share the same message and are able to act on it, usually the more the diffusion, the more effective the message. Boisot (1987) argues that effectiveness is unrelated to the level of codification, since people can act on uncodified messages as they can act on codified messages. There is no direct relationship between level of codification and effectiveness. Hence line *C* is shown as perpendicular, and can move left or right.

It is one of the assumptions in this text that as the level of codification increases, the sharing of information can be facilitated, providing the code is easy enough to learn quickly and that the analogy (the code) is credible and acceptable. It is perhaps the task of psychology to suitably codify common-sense experience so as to make it possible to be shared and subject to analysis by comparison across a particular population (see Chapter One on the criteria of a science). However by so doing (ie creating a suitable analogy which allows codification), the psychologist will always be simplifying experience and possibly reducing it to banal levels.

In a commercial situation money is a code which is shared, and as we have argued elsewhere (Jackson, 1989), represents the need to demonstrate performance of human resources in cash terms.

The credibility and acceptability factors of the code are related to the character of the culture, which can be described by the two dimensions of codification and diffusion. We can refer back to our bi-polar cultural model (p. 159), introducing Boisot's (1987) two dimensions into it.

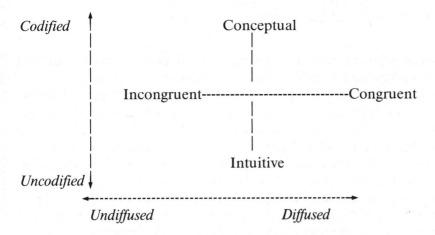

The bi-polar dimension of conceptual-intuitive is a descriptive characteristic of the culture, which relates to the uncodified-codified continuum of Boisot (1987). The incongruent-congruent dimension is a developmental characteristic of the culture, indicating the 'strength' of the culture or the sharing of values and rules, the ideal development route from less to more sharing of assumptions, values and rules, and having implications for the performance of the organization concerned. This is directly related to the undiffused-diffused continuum of Boisot (1987).

A conceptual style of management would use codified information, and would favour codification in conceptualizing and acting. The pragmatic, intuitive management style would favour less conceptualization, and therefore less codification. 'Common sense' ideas would prevail in this type of culture, rather than highly codified knowledge.

A congruent culture, representing a high level of sharing of meaning, would occur where there is good interpersonal communication within the organization. A congruent style of management would occur where there is good intrapersonal communication (that is the manager has a high degree of self-awareness and self-organization).

The codification and diffusion differences within a corporate culture have implications for three methodological issues:

- methods used for measuring performance;
- reliability and validity of measurement;
- development implications of the measurement.

We can relate these issues to the communication problems outlined by Shannon and Weaver (1947) and illustrated by Boisot (1989).
1. *Technical problem*. We can say that the higher the degree of coding of cultural information within an organization (conceptual management), the easier it will be to share this information with an outsider who knows the codes (curve A). Conversely, the less codified the cultural information, the more difficult it will be to share the information. It is also more likely to be easier to obtain acceptability for a lengthy questionnaire seeking quantitative information, to obtain face validity of the instrument, and to obtain reliable data, if the cultural information in the organization is highly codified and managers are used to dealing with this level of codification. It is also likely to provide information which makes sense to the organization, which will help development in the areas which have been measured. If we refer to line *A* (p. 178), a measurement initiative is more likely to be successful in the top right-hand of the cultural space (rational management in the model on p. 159).

Other, less structured (and perhaps qualitative) approaches are more likely to be successful in the bottom left hand of the cultural space (line *A*). However, Shannon and Weaver's Semantic problem adds another dimension to this.

2. *Semantic problem*. We have seen that line *B* represents the audience which is capable of understanding a message. This shows that the more the message is coded the less people will understand it. We could also say that the more coded, the harder it is to share the message if the audience does not agree on, or share, the required codes. As an example, if you keep the issue of management performance in an organization at an uncodified level, there may be misunderstandings from time to time but not conscious disagreements until you try to make tangible measures for performance. So when specific issues such as appraisal and reward, or appraisal and disciplinary procedures against a poor performer come to the fore, there may be disagreements as to how it is possible to measure performance, and what that

performance actually is. Similarly, if a consultant goes into an organization and tries to measure management performance quantitatively, there may be disagreements regarding the measures of performance unless agreement and understanding can be reached on what constitutes a performance measure.

Generally speaking, the less sharing of information in an organization about performance criteria and performance level – owing to poor feedback and poor communication generally – the worse the agreement on performance if highly codified measurement techniques are used.

Looking at the cultural space through which line *B* is going (p. 179), at its top left we are likely to obtain codified information through questionnaires, but it will not be very reliable as there will be little sharing and agreement on the code used. At the bottom right, we are likely to get fairly reliable results with less structured methods of data collection. Note that it is possible to get internal reliability through split-half methods, but not to get agreement between co-raters who are co-workers of the subject manager. This indicates an incongruent situation.

So if we collect structured data on a manager's performance using a questionnaire given to the manager and his or her co-workers, we are likely to get agreement to the right of our cultural space (congruent) and disagreement at the left of our cultural space (incongruent, see p. 159).

3. *Effectiveness problem.* The problem of effectiveness is addressed by gaining a basic understanding of the type of culture you are dealing with, and using appropriate methods. Line *C* (p. 180) shows that this is unrelated to the level of codification, but that a measure of the level of effectiveness is a position along the bottom axis of our cultural space, or along the undiffused-diffused continuum: the more diffused the message, the more effective it is. This would certainly be the case in measuring performance, particularly as we are looking at it as a vehicle for developing agreement on performance in an organization.

Unfortunately, Boisot (1987) provides very little direct help on how to measure variation along the two dimensions of the cultural space. He suggests a concept of measurement for the codification dimension, where on a scale of 0 – 1 we can describe to what extent a message can be compressed into symbols. This uses the reciprocal of the number of binary digits (bits) which are needed to transmit the message, where 0 equals 1/infinity, or 0 represents the condition where no number of symbols can exhaust the message. 1/1 represents a situation where a message of any length can be compressed into one symbol. We can therefore see that financial data would figure towards the top of the scale, and personal values and feelings would figure towards the bottom.

Boisot's (1987) help on the diffusion scale is equally vague. He suggests a scale of the percentage of a given population receiving a message. However, in practice this must be difficult to precisely measure outside laboratory conditions.

A far more valuable concept of a diffusion scale would be based on the agreement of a particular population on a particular message. For example we could ask a number of co-workers in an organization to rank their organization's criteria for management performance and look at the correlation (or variance) in their respective rankings. We could also ask several co-workers to rate the performance of a manager and look at the variance in their ratings. This would give a measure on a diffusion scale ranging from 100 per cent agreement to no agreement.

The problem of measurement of the levels of codification and of diffusion, however, relates back to the discussion in the previous pages. To measure we need to codify, and to codify we need the co-operation of a population which can be placed towards the conceptual end of our continuum. Therefore, it is only really possible (using this theorem) to measure the level of codification, and diffusion, when we are measuring a high level of codification. This is not a problem, as far as the present author is aware, which has been tackled head on before, but is a problem which relates directly to the approach to measurement as communication.

We have therefore said that a high level of codification may not be appropriate in all organizational contexts, and that particularly, we would not expect intuitive style managers to be highly responsive to this approach. We have begun to provide an analogy of a cultural framework for exploring communication management, and we will now look specifically at this framework in order to describe stylistic differences and process problems. We will then explore a methodological approach which gains valuable information about managers' positioning within this framework.

The process continuum: incongruent–congruent

This continuum is important for measuring management performance for two main reasons:

- it indicates the effectiveness of communication within an organizational unit by measuring the amount of agreement on information available on an individual manager;
- it provides a way of dealing with the very real problems of reliability of information obtained, inter-rater reliability, and convergent validity of the instruments used when attempting to measure management performance.

We have outlined in previous chapters the importance of communication to the function of management, and that above all else (following Mintzberg, 1973) this is the way in which managers achieve results. Communication within an organization is complex, and the facilitation and sharing of information and attitudes involves an understanding of organizational context, the content of communication, and the conduct or skills of communication. However despite this complexity, a measure of agreement on performance criteria, actual performance, and management style can be obtained, which indicates the 'fit' of communication, or the congruence (consistency, or amount of sharing of information) in a particular organizational unit.

The present author has used the management analysis questionnaire to measure this 'fit', and we will be describing this shortly.

The stylistic continuum: intuitive–conceptual

Essentially, this continuum measures the culture of an organizational unit as well as the style of individual managers. A useful comparison is the 'fit' between the style of the individual manager, and the prevailing style which reflects the culture of the unit.

This continuum reflects the degree of coding of information used in managing the enterprize, including feedback on performance and the general ideas which people have about performance in the organization.

THE MANAGEMENT ANALYSIS QUESTIONNAIRE (MAQ)

The MAQ was designed specifically for conceptual managers in order to measure their analogous position on both dimensions – incongruent–congruent and intuitive–conceptual and to feed back this information for development purposes. Other methods are being developed for intuitive managers, and there is some overlap. The view expressed in the preceding pages – that intuitive managers do not like completing questionnaires – is a fairly mechanistic statement, yet can be regarded as a general rule. Such methods as observation and shadowing provide qualitative information usually sufficient to determine whether the manager is intuitive or conceptual, but not enough information to determine his or her location along the incongruent-congruent continuum. Such methods as critical incident reports, and variations of the Thematic Apperception Test described in Chapter 7, can be used, providing that co-workers' perceptions of the subject managers are incorporated within the information collected.

The questionnaires are given to the manager, his or her immediate supervisor, one peer – a colleague of the same organizational level who knows the work of the manager but does not report to, nor is reported to by, the manager – and two subordinates. The differences between the average scores of the co-workers and the subject manager is an indication of position along the inconguent–congruent continuum.

The questionnaire measures both style and perceived performance, and is designed, as follows, using the method of questionnaire design outlined in Chapter 3.

Firstly, in the main body of the questionnaire there are three separate tests: *style*, measuring the dimension conceptual–intuitive; personal *orientation*, measuring a perception of the incongruent-congruent dimension; and *performance*, measuring the perceptions of the manager on the dimension of high-low performer.

The content areas (please refer to Chapter 3 for the terms used) for style and orientation are as follows.

Style		**Orientation**	
Conceptual	Intuitive	Congruent	Incongruent

The manifestations (see Chapter 3) are:

- way they learn;
- way they work;
- way they relate to others;
- way they relate to the future;
- how they regard performance.

For example, items written for *conceptual* and the 'way they learn' are: 'Completing questionnaires can be useful', and 'I learn best from reading and attending courses'; while the equivalent items for *intuitive* were 'Completing questionnaires is generally a waste of time', and 'I learn best from doing the job'.

For performance, the content areas were high performance and low performance, with the manifestations being:

- demonstration of skills and knowledge;
- demonstration of motivation;
- results achieved in current job;
- perceived reaction to and use made of change;
- perceived future potential.

Items indicating high performance, by a demonstration of skills and knowledge are: 'Has finely tuned management skills', and 'Has good knowledge of both job and people'; where the low performance indicators were 'Does not demonstrate a high level of management skills', and 'Does not show a good knowledge of job nor of people'.

Respondents are also asked to rank a list of criteria for performance (this is discussed in Chapter 5). The questionnaire starts with personal details and an indication of make-up of the job, which is fully discussed in Chapter 4.

The manager's questionnaire is as follows, with a similar questionnaire going to the co-workers.

Please complete the following details.

Name .... Position ....

Section/Branch ....

How long in current position? .... How long with the company? ....

Age (tick as appropriate) 20s[ ] 30s[ ] 40s[ ] 50s[ ] 60s[ ]

Address for correspondence ....

....

To give an idea of what your job entails, please allocate your time between the activities below. For each activity circle the appropriate percentage.

CIRCLE APPROPRIATE %

1. Technical/professional
   activities concerned
   with your specialization   10 20 30 40 50 60 70 80 90 100
2. Selling/promoting/PR   10 20 30 40 50 60 70 80 90 100
3. Planning   10 20 30 40 50 60 70 80 90 100
4. Implementing decisions   10 20 30 40 50 60 70 80 90 100
5. Developing staff   10 20 30 40 50 60 70 80 90 100
6. Controlling/co-ordinating   10 20 30 40 50 60 70 80 90 100
7. Troubleshooting/problem
   solving   10 20 30 40 50 60 70 80 90 100
8. Rewarding performance   10 20 30 40 50 60 70 80 90 100
9. Obtaining direct results   10 20 30 40 50 60 70 80 90 100
10. Other (please specify)

    ....   10 20 30 40 50 60 70 80 90 100

Total should add up to 100%

Briefly describe the objectives of your job.

....

....

....

For each item below tick (✔) the box if you agree more than you disagree. Put a cross (X) in the box if you disagree more than you agree.

[ ]   1.   I don't like to pre-judge people, but to reflect on them for some time

[ ]   2.   I tend to plan carefully before I act

[ ]   3.   I make quick judgements about people

[ ]   4.   Results are more important than the way they are achieved

[ ]   5.   Completing questionnaires can be really useful

[ ]   6.   I plan strategically, step by step, for the future

[   ]   7.   I thrive on change

[   ]   8.   The way you achieve results is as important as the results themselves

[   ]   9.   I generally work 'by the seat of my pants'

[   ]   10.   I learn best from reading and attending courses

[   ]   11.   Completing questionnaires is generally a waste of time

[   ]   12.   Psychological theory can help us understand about other people

[   ]   13.   I deliberate a great deal about my job and the way I do it

[   ]   14.   Goal setting for the future is more important than strategic step-by-step planning

[   ]   15.   Good education and training is more important to good performance than is a manager's instincts

[   ]   16.   I learn best from doing the job

[   ]   17.   I tend to take things as they come

[   ]   18.   Psychological theory has no bearing on the way I work with people

[   ]   19.   Stability is as important as change

[   ]   20.   A manager's instincts are more important than education and training for a manager's performance

[   ]   21.   I have little idea of what the future holds

[   ]   22.   I am consistent in my methods of working

[   ]   23.   I learn in a systematic way

[   ]   24.   I seem to learn in an *ad hoc* way

[   ]   25.   I have a clear vision of the future

[   ]   26.   I am very clear about what constitutes good management performance

[   ]   27.   I am not very open in my dealings with people

[   ]   28.   My method of working is often haphazard and inconsistent

[ ] 29. I approach my work in a systematic way

[ ] 30. I am not thoroughly clear on how to manage change for the future

[ ] 31. I do not communicate a clear idea of what I feel is good performance to my subordinates

[ ] 32. I am open in my dealings with people

[ ] 33. I share my learning experiences with others

[ ] 34. I understand clearly how to manage change for the future

[ ] 35. I am unclear about what constitutes good management performance

[ ] 36. I am a good communicator

[ ] 37. I approach work in a systematic way

[ ] 38. I communicate a clear idea of what performance is required from subordinates

[ ] 39. I often feel I do not communicate very well

[ ] 40. I do not tend to pass on my learning and experience to others

[ ] 41. I am regarded as a high achiever in the results I obtain in my job

[ ] 42. I tend not to be up to date with current initiatives and changes

[ ] 43. I have a good knowledge of both job and people

[ ] 44. I tend to lead change rather than follow on behind

[ ] 45. I would not say I have a high level of management skills

[ ] 46. I will do very well in this organization

[ ] 47. I have a high degree of motivation in everything I undertake

[ ] 48. I see change as a threat

[ ] 49. I motivate others

[ ] 50. I am regarded as a high flier

[ ] 51. I would say that my results as a manager have not been outstanding

[ ] 52. I generally do not have a high degree of motivation in the work I undertake

[ ] 53. I do not think I will do particularly well in this organization

[ ] 54. I have finely tuned management skills

[ ] 55. I would not describe myself as a high achiever in the results I obtain in my job

[ ] 56. I see change as a challenge and as an opportunity

[ ] 57. I am not regarded as a high flier

[ ] 58. I have obtained very good results as a manager

[ ] 59. I often have difficulty motivating others

[ ] 60. My knowledge of the job and of people I work with could be considerably improved

You are now asked to rank the following ten criteria of management perform-ance in order of importance in your organization. 1 is the most important, 10 is the least important.

		[Rank 1 – 10]
A.	Having good knowledge of the job	[ ]
B.	Contributing to profits	[ ]
C.	Getting the days work done	[ ]
D.	Motivating staff	[ ]
E.	Contributing to organizational growth and development for the future	[ ]
F.	Obtaining optimum productivity through staff	[ ]
G.	Developing staff	[ ]
H.	Contributing to organizational stability	[ ]
I.	Managing change	[ ]
J.	Solving problems and making decisions	[ ]

The information fed back to the manager regards his or her position along the stylistic continuum and the high-low performance continuum (self-perception), compared with co-workers collective perception. It is difficult to feed back information from individual co-workers because of the need for confidentiality when co-workers complete the questionnaires. Even so, a suggestion may be made to the managers that they would be wise to discuss differences in perceptions where these are great. This is often the beginning of a fruitful exchange which breaks down hitherto existing barriers of communication, of which the managers may not have been aware.

The organizational unit head is also made aware of the differences in perceptions along the incongruent-congruent continuum. This is particularly pertinent where there are great differences. A good indicator of performance problems is the performance criteria list. Where there are major differences in the rank order of the list, there is need for the management team to get together and agree criteria.

SOME CONCLUSIONS

Let us now try to draw together the ideas discussed in this text. The intention has been to provide a framework and basis from which to look at the measurement of management performance. This task was undertaken in Section One. Section Two sought to describe some of the work that had been undertaken in this field, particularly with regard to the different factors in management performance. Section Three then introduced an approach to measurement, drawing on the information and ideas in the previous sections.

We discussed measurement as essentially an act of communication, relying on a representation of reality (an analogy), and impacting on those that are measured through feedback. It is perhaps only by treating measurement like this that we can achieve the scientific objectives outlined in Chapter 1 as our criteria for a scientific study of management performance.

By focusing on the perceptions of individual managers in relation to others' perceptions of them, we have played a valuable part in the discovery of what may not have otherwise been discovered (criterion one). The approach has mainly been derived from common sense approaches of managers, which have in fact been two different types of common sense: intuitive and conceptual (criterion two). To a large extent, we are trying to change managers' perceptions (criterion three), to give them more control of their environment by giving them feedback on that environment (criterion four), and allowing them to take the necessary action to correct problems such as those of communication. We can also provide a control for bias and group conformity by using triangulation (see Chapter Three) in this method (criterion five). We are also at the stage of addressing the problems of validity (criterion six). Logically, if information is generated which is acceptable to managers and is useful in a developmental process, then the techniques used to generate the information are valid! This may seem slightly naive, but it works in a practical management situation. The approach which has been taken can be summarized as follows.

In order to help analyse management performance in its various aspects we developed a descriptive model (the 3 Cs) which categorized information about management performance into *context*, *content* and *conduct*, and provided the basis of discussion for three theoretical frameworks (paradigms) which underpin the three

Criteria	Approach
1. Discover what would otherwise be hidden	Provide an analogy of management performance to help explain processes and results Focus on perceptions of others as well as managers to provide a view of 'shared meaning'
2. Start from common sense	Derive analogy from the way managers see themselves relating this to every-day experience through the categories of *intuitive* and *conceptual* management Discover skills language of organization

Criteria	Approach
3. Change cognitive frame-work on which actions are based	Provide feedback on performance and others' perception to allow a negotiation of their cognitive framework upon which they can act
4. Enable managers to gain control over processes and thus produce results they would not otherwise produce	Provide the basis of necessary action such as training, team development, etc, through feedback (see 3. above)
5. Take account of bias	Use perceptions of co-workers to provide triangulation
6. Be shown to be valid	Is the analogy and information generated acceptable to managers? Is it useful as a basis for action? Does it help the development process? Does it *work* in practice?

Figure 9.2 *Summary of approaches taken to measure management performance*

categories: namely, structuralism (context), phenomenology (content) and behaviourism (conduct).

These frameworks (described in Chapter 2) led to much of the descriptive work in Section Two, as follows.

- *Context*: structure, rules, technology – Chapters 4, 6.
- *Content*: perceptions, motives, attitudes – Chapters 6, 7.
- *Conduct*: Skills, behaviours – Chapters 4, 5.

This provided descriptions and discussion on work already carried out in the area of management performance measurement, giving practical illustrations where this was appropriate.

Finally, in Section Three we offered an analogy to provide a route through the sometimes confusing debate about management competencies. This analogy builds on the work done in Sections One and Two and is based on:

- an idea of what constitutes a scientific method;
- a conceptual framework of management as communication;
- a concept of measurement as communication.

It provides a combination of context, content (prevailing organizational culture and management styles, or managers' interpretations of their role and conduct), and conduct (what managers actually do, results they achieve, and what skills they need in order to achieve results within a particular context).

Thus we developed the two dimensions of intuitive-conceptual (styles, interpretations and perceptions: that is, content within a specific context), and congruent-incongruent (what managers actually do, particularly communication within a team setting: that is, conduct within a particular context).

One of the points we stressed is that measurement is in fact a form of communication. Any analogy (content), which represents the reality of a situation (context and conduct) within an organization, must be accepted in practice by those who will be involved with it as part of a development process (conduct). It is no good positing an analogy if the interested managers will not accept it as being practically useful. There is a need therefore to provide a balance between an analogy being too complex, so nobody will understand it, and being too simple so that it is useless. This is what we have tried to do here by focusing on two broad dimensions to which managers can relate. However, social reality is very complex and there is always the danger that we will miss some of the complexity of an actual management situation.

There is no denying that much fine tuning has to be done with this basic analogy (developed in this chapter and Chapter 8) and in some cases, further sub-dimensions might be pursued which have a bearing on management situations in various contexts.

The advice we would give here to any reader who wishes to use this model of management performance, or any other model for that matter, within an organization, is to work on it with the managers concerned. Share it with them, discuss it, fine tune it, get them to adopt it as their own. Without this, without acceptance of the model, you will not get co-operation from the managers with whom you are working. Remember, the value of any scientific approach is that it begins where common sense is *now*, and develops on that common sense. If you want to take managers with you, build on *their* common sense, not your own!

We have spent a long time in this text discussing theory, but theory which is entrenched in the day-to-day activities of management, and which has largely grown from the problems of measuring managers who do not want to be measured: a practical theory! This certainly is not the end of the story. There is a long way to go in developing both measurement instruments and development programmes for intuitive managers: the vast majority of measurement techniques and development tools and programmes are geared to the needs of the *conceptual* manager.

There is no doubt that managers are different. They may require the same general competencies in order to perform, but these competencies may be manifested quite differently in the performance. To regard all managers as the same is fruitless, as is regarding all managers as completely different. By developing and using a model or analogy of the reality of management, we can better develop the necessary tools to measure and manage managers, and help managers to manage. This text may have helped to point the way.

Bibliography

Aiken, L R (1988) *Psychological Testing and Assessment* Boston: Allyn and Bacon

Alderfer, C P (1972) *Existence, Relatedness and Growth: Human Needs in Organizational Settings* New York: Free Press

Alliger, G M and Janak, E A (1989) 'Kirkpatrick's levels of training criteria: thirty years later' in *Personnel Psychology* 42, pp. 331–42

Anastasi, A (1988) *Psychological Testing* New York: Macmillan

Argyle, M (1967) *The Psychology of Interpersonal Behaviour* Harmondsworth: Penguin

Argyle, M, Furnham, A and Graham, J A (1981) *Social Situations* Cambridge: CUP

Argyris, C and Schon, D (1978) *Organizational Learning* Massachusetts: Addison-Wesley

Berger, P L and Luckmann, T (1966) *The Social Construction of Reality* New York: Doubleday

Berne, E (1964) *Games People Play* Harmondsworth: Penguin

Blake, R R and Mouton, J S (1985) *The Managerial Grid III* Houston: Gulf

Blau, P (1964) *Exchange and Power in Social Life* New York: John Wiley

Boisot, M (1987) *Information and Organizations: The manager as anthropologist* London: Collins/Fontana

Breakwell, G M, Foot, H and Gilmour, R (1988) *Doing Social Psychology* Cambridge: CUP

Brianas, J (1986) 'Management styles: a matter of statistical probability' in *Training and Development*, October

Brown, J A C (1954) *The Social Psychology of Industry* Harmondsworth: Penguin

Burns, R B (1979) *The Self Concept* London: Longman

Cameron, K S (1980) 'Critical questions in assessing organizational effectiveness' in *Organizational Dynamics* 9, No. 2 (autumn) pp. 66–80

Campbell, J P et al (1970) *Managerial Behaviour, Performance and Effectiveness* New York: McGraw-Hill

Campbell, J P and Pritchard, R D (1976) 'Motivational theory in industrial and organizational psychology' in Dunnette, M D (ed.) *Handbook of Industrial and Organizational Psychology* Chicago: Rand McNally

Carson, R C (1969) *Interaction Concepts of Personality* Harmondsworth: Penguin

Cascio, W F and Ramos, R A (1986) 'Development and application of a new method for assessing job performance in behavioural/economic terms' in *Journal of Applied Psychology* Vol. 71, No. 1, pp. 20–28

Cherry, C (1957) *On Human Communication* Massachusetts: MIT Press

Cirourel, A V (1964), *Method and Measurement in Sociology* New York: The Free Press

Cline, V (1964) 'Interpersonal perceptions' in Maher, B A (ed.) *Progress in Experimental Research, Vol. 1* New York: Academic Press

Cockerill, T (1989) 'The kind of competence for rapid change' in *Personnel Management*, September

Cohen, A R and Bradford, D L (1989) 'Influence without authority: the use of alliances, reciprocity and exchange to accomplish work' in *Organizational Dynamics*, winter

Cohen, L and Holliday, M (1982) *Statistics For Social Scientists* London: Harper and Row

Cohen, L and Manion, L (1980) *Research Methods in Education* London: Croom Helm

Cook, M (1988) 'Person perception' in Breakwell et al (1988)

Cooley, C H (1902) *Human Nature and the Social Order* New York: Charles Scribner

Coonradt, C A (1984) *The Game of Work* Salt Lake City: Shadow Mountain

Cronbach, L J (1984) *Essentials of Psychological Testing* New York: Harper and Row

Cronbach, L J and Meehl, P E (1955) 'Construct validity in psychological tests' in *Psychological Bulletin* 52, pp. 177–94

Danziger, K, (1976) *Interpersonal Communication* New York: Pergamon

Dulewicz, V (1989) 'Assessment centres as a route to competence' in *Personnel Management*, November

Durkheim, E (1915) *The Elementary Forms of the Religious Life* (trans. Swain, J W) London: Allen and Unwin

Eysenck, H J (1970) *The Structure of Human Personality* London: Methuen

Fiedler, F (1967) *A Theory of Leadership Effectiveness* New York: McGraw-Hill

Fiske, J (1982) *Introduction to Communication Studies* London: Methuen

Fleishman, E A and Quaintance, M K (1984) *Taxonomy of Human Performance* New York: Academic Press

Forgas, J P, Argyle, M and Ginsberg, G P (1981) 'Person perception and the interaction episode' in Argyle et al (1981)

Garratt, B (1987) *The Learning Organization* London: Fontana/Collins

Ghiselli, E E (1971) *Explorations in Managerial Talent* Calif: Goodyear

Gibb, C A (1954) 'Leadership' in Lindzey, G (ed.) *Handbook of Social Psychology* Reading, Mass: Addison-Wesley

Glaze, T (1989) 'Cadbury's dictionary of competence' in *Personnel Management*, July

Goffman, E (1959) *The Presentation of Self in Everyday Life* Harmondsworth: Penguin (1971 edition)

Greatrex, J and Phillips, P (1989) 'Oiling the wheels of competence' in *Personnel Management*, August

Halliday, M A K (1970) 'Language structure and language function' in Lyon, J (ed.) *New Horizons in Linguistics* Harmondsworth: Penguin

Harré, R (1981) 'The positive-empiricist approach and its alternatives' in Reason, P and Rowan, J, *Human Enquiry* Chichester: John Wiley

Harré, R (1988) 'Ethnogenic methods: an empirical psychology of action' in Breakwell et al (1988)

Harré, R, Clarke, D and DeCarlo, N (1985), *Motives and Mechanisms* London: Methuen

Harris, T (1967) *I'm Okay, You're Okay* New York: Harper and Row

Heckhausen, H (1963) *Hoffnung und Furcht in der Leistungsmotivation* Meisenheim, W Germany: Hain, quoted in McClelland, 1987

Heider, F (1958) *The Psychology of Interpersonal Relations* New York: Wiley

Herriot, P (1988) 'Managerial assessment: the research evidence – Appendix 1, in Hirsh, W and Bevan, S (1988)

Hersey, P and Blanchard, K (1977) *Organizational Behaviour: Utilizing Human Resources* Englewood Cliff, New Jersey: Prentice-Hall

Herzberg, F, Mausner, B and Snyderman, B (1959) *The Motivation to Work* New York: Wiley

Hirsh W, and Bevan, S (1988) *What Makes a Manager?* Brighton: Institute of Manpower Studies

Hirsh, W (1989) *Defining Managerial Skills* Brighton: Institute of Manpower Studies

Hodge, B J and Anthony, W P (1988) *Organizational Theory* Boston: Allyn and Bacon

Hofstede, G (1989) 'Organizing for cultural diversity' in *European Management Journal* Vol. 7, No. 4.

Holding, D H (1965) *Principles of Training* London: Pergamon

Holt, J (1976) *Instead of Education* Harmondsworth: Penguin

Homans, G (1958) 'Social behaviour as exchange' in *American Journal of Sociology* 63, pp. 597–606

Honey, P and Mumford, A (1982) *The Manual of Learning Styles* Maidenhead: Peter Honey

Hurd, D L and Kipling, J J (eds) (1964) *The Origins and Growth of the Physical Sciences, Vol.1* Harmondsworth: Penguin

Hurst, D K (1986) 'Why strategic management is bankrupt' in *Organizational Dynamics*, autumn

Ilgen, D R, Fisher, C D and Taylor, M S (1979) 'Consequences of individual feedback on behaviour in organizations' in *Journal of Applied Psychology* 64 (4), pp. 340–71

Jackson, L (1989) 'Turning airport managers into high fliers' in *Personnel Management*, October

Jackson, T (1984) *Interpersonal Communication: Education and Training in Business Studies* unpublished Master's thesis, Keele University

Jackson, T (1989) *Evaluation: Relating Training to Business Performance* London: Kogan Page

Jacobs, R (1989) 'Getting the measure of management competence' in *Personnel Management*, June

James, W (1892) 'The social self' reprinted in Stone and Faberman (eds) (1970) *Social Psychology Through Symbolic Interactionism* Waltham, Massachusetts: Xerox College Publishing

Johnson, D W and Johnson, F P (1975), *Joining Together: Group Theory and*

Group Skills Englewood Cliff, New Jersey: Prentice-Hall

Johnson, T J , Feigenbaum, R and Weiby, M (1964) 'Some determinants and consequences of the teacher's perceptions of causation' in *Journal of Educational Psychology* 55, pp. 237–46

Kakabadse, A, Ludlow, R and Vinnicombe, S (1987) *Working in Organizations* Harmondsworth: Penguin

Katz, D and Kahn, R L, (1978) *The Social Psychology of Organizations* (second edn) New York: John Wiley

Kelley, H H (1967) 'Attribution theory in social psychology' in *Nebraska Symposium on Motivation* 15, pp. 192–238

Kelley, H H (1973) 'The processes of causal attribution' in *American Psychologist*, 28, pp. 107–28

Kelly, G A (1955) *The Psychology of Personal Constructs, Vols 1 and 2* New York: Norton

Kimura, Y and Yoshimori, M (1989) 'Japan imports american management methods through an MBA programme' in *Journal of Management Development* 8, 4

Kline, P (1986) *A Handbook of Test Construction* London: Methuen, 1986

Komaki, J, Heinzmann, A T and Lawson, L (1980) 'Effects of training and feedback: component analysis of a behavioral safety programme' in *Journal of Applied Psychology* 65, pp. 261–70

Lalljee, M (1988) 'Attribution processes' in Breakwell et al (1988)

Lessem, R (1989) *Global Management Principles* London: Prentice-Hall

Lewin, K (1947) 'Group decision making and social change' in Newcombe, T M, Hartley, E L, et al (1947) *Readings in Social Psychology* New York: Henry Holt, pp. 330–44

Likert, R (1967) *The Human Organization* Tokyo: McGraw-Hill Kogakusha

McArthur, L R and Barron, R M (1983) 'Towards an ecological theory of social perception' in *Psychological Review* 90, pp. 215–38

McClelland, D C (1987) *Human Motivation* Cambridge: CUP

Maccoby, M (1976) *The Gamesman* New York: Simon and Schuster

McCormick, E J and Ilgen, D (1985) *Industrial and Organizational Psychology* London: Allen and Unwin

McEnery, J and McEnery, J M, (1987) 'Self-rating in management training needs assessment: a neglected opportunity?' in *Journal of Occupational Psychology* 60, pp. 49–60

McGregor, D (1960) *The Human Side of Enterprise* New York: McGraw-Hill

Maslow, A H (1954) *Motivation of Personality* New York: Harper and Row

Mead, G H (1934) *Mind, Self and Society* Chicago: University of Chicago Press

Miller, R B (1953) *Handbook on Training and Training Equipment Design* Wright Air Development Centre, Technical Report WADC-TR-53-136, cited in Ribeaux and Poppleton (1978)

Miller, D T and Ross, M (1975) 'Self-serving biases in the attribution of causality: fact or fiction?' *Psychological Bulletin* 82, pp. 213–25

Miner, J B (1978) *The Management Process* New York: Macmillan

Mintzberg, H (1973) *The Nature of Managerial Work* Englewood Cliff, New Jersey: Prentice-Hall

Morgan, R G T (1979) 'Analysis of social skills: the behaviour analysis approach' in Singleton, Spurgeon and Stammers (eds) (1979)

Morse, N C and Reimer, E (1956) 'The experimental change of a major organizational variable' in *Journal of Abnormal and Social Psychology* 52, pp. 120–29

Mullins, L and Aldrich, P (1988) 'An integrated model of management and managerial development' in *Journal of Management Development* 7, 3,

Murray, H A (1938) *Explorations in Personality* New York: Oxford University Press

Myers, M T and Myers G E (1982) *Managing By Communication: An Organizational Approach*, New York: McGraw-Hill

Newcomb, T (1953) 'An approach to the study of communication acts' in *Psychological Review* 60

Newcomb, T (1959) 'Individual systems of orientation' in Koch, S (ed.) *Psychology: A Study of a Science* New York: McGraw-Hill

Parsons, T (1949) *The Structure of Social Action* Illinois: Glencoe

Porter, L W and Lawler, E E III (1968) *Managerial Attitudes and Performance* Illinois: Dorsey Press

Prien, E (1977) 'The function of job analysis in content validation' in *Personnel Psychology* 30, pp. 167–74

Pritchard, R D , Jones S D et al (1989) 'The evaluation of an integrated approach to measuring organizational productivity' in *Personnel Psychology* 42, pp. 69–115

Rackham, N, Honey, P and Colbert, M et al (1971) *Developing Interactive Skills* Northampton: Wellens Publishing

Radcliffe-Brown, A R (1952) *Structure and Function in Primitive Society* London: Cohen and West

Reason P and Rowan J (eds) (1981) *Human Inquiry: A Sourcebook of New Paradigm Research* Chichester, U K: John Wiley

Reddin, W J (1970) *Managerial Effectiveness* London: McGraw-Hill

Reddin W J (1989) 'Expressing effectiveness in terms of outputs' in *Personnel Management*, October

Ribeaux, P and Poppleton, S E (1978) *Psychology and Work: An Introduction* Basingstoke: Macmillan

Rogers, C R (1951) *Client Centred Therapy* Boston, USA: Houghton Mufflin

Roloff, M E (1981) *Interpersonal Communication: The Social Exchange Approach* Beverly Hills: Sage

Rotter, J B (1966) 'Generalized expectancies for internal versus external control of reinforcement' *Psychological Monographs* 80, 1, whole No. 609

Rowbottom, R (1977) *Social Analysis* London: Heinemann

Rust, J and Golombok, S (1989) *Modern Psychometrics: The Science of Psychological Assessment* London: Routledge

Sanford, N (1981) 'A model for action research' in Reason and Rowan (1981)

Schein, E H (1985) *Organizational Culture and Leadership*, San Fransisco: Jossey-Bass

Schutz, A (1972) *Phenomenology of the Social World* London: Heinemann

Shannon, C E and Weaver, W (1949) *The Mathematical Theory of Communication* Illinois: University of Illinois Press

Silverman, D (1970) *The Theory of Organizations* London: Heinemann

Singleton, W T, Spurgeon, P and Stammers, R B (eds) (1979) *The Analysis of Social Skills* New York: Plenum Press

Skinner, B F (1953) *Science and Human Behaviour* New York: Macmillan

Smiley, T (1989) 'A challenge to the human resources and organizational function in international firms' in *European Management Journal* Vol. 7., No. 2

Spencer, L M (1986) *Calculating Human Resource Costs and Benefits* New York: John Wiley

Stewart, D (1986) *The Power of People Skills* New York: John Wiley

Stewart, R (1985) *The Reality of Management* London: Pan Books (2nd edn)

Tannenbaum, R and Schmitt, W H (1973) 'How to choose a leadership pattern' in *Harvard Business Review*, May/June

Torrington, D and Weightman, J (1985) *The Business of Management* Englewood Cliff, New Jersey: Prentice-Hall

Tsui, A S and Ohlott, P (1988) 'Multiple assessment of managerial effectiveness: interrater agreement and consensus in effectiveness models' in *Personnel Psychology* 41, pp. 779–803

Tylor, E B (1871) *Primitive Culture,* cited in Levi-Strauss, C (1963) *Structural Anthropology* trans: Jacobson, C and Schoel, B G Harmondsworth: Penguin

Vroom, V H (1964) *Work and Motivation* New York: Wiley

Weiner, N (1948) *Cybernetics* Massachusetts: The MIT Press

Williams, A, Dobson, P and Walters, M (1989) *Changing Culture* London: Institute of Personnel Management

Wohler, A J, and London, M (1989) 'Ratings of managerial characteristics, evaluation difficulties, co-worker agreement and self-awareness' *Personnel Psychology* 42, pp. 235–61

SOFTWARE

MYSTAT: An instruction version of SYSTAT for the PC, SYSTAT Inc, 1800 Sherman Avenue, Evanston, IL 60201

SPSS: SPSS UK Ltd, SPSS House, London Street, Chertsey, Surrey KT16 8AP

Index